Our God Reigns

Our God Reigns

John Coventry, S.J.

Sheed & Ward

London

ISBN 0 7220 6380 6

Published in Great Britain in 1995 by
Sheed & Ward Limited
14 Coopers Row
London EC3N 2BH

Production editor Bill Ireson
Printed and bound by Biddles Ltd, Guildford, Surrey

Contents

Our God Reigns

PART ONE

Some Basics

Origin of the Gospels

Authorship

The ancients did not have our twentieth-century idea of authorship. For example, modern scholarship discloses that the book of Isaiah belongs to three periods before and during the exile of the Jews in Babylon.

The book is, in fact, divided into three parts (Is 1–39, 40–55, and 56–66). Later writers, belonging to a 'school' of Isaiah, wrote under the mantle of Isaiah. Another example is to be found in the New Testament epistles, Timothy, 2 Peter, and Titus: someone at a later date, after the death of the apostle, was writing under his aegis. So, too, for Colossians and Ephesians. We can conclude, therefore, that the *community* is the author of the gospels. It seems that, regarding the coming of Jesus, the community first looked forward before they looked back.

Much work has been done by scholars to distinguish the proclamation (*kerygma*) from the teaching (*didache*). Paul is our earliest witness, and he shows little interest in anything Jesus said or did (*cf* 1 Cor 7:10). Mark's gospel is generally recognized to be the earliest (*c*69–70 AD), and it shows the arrangement of traditional material in 'sections' (*pericopae*), the teaching of Mark's community and the clear stamp of one mind (our chapters and verses being much later). So, too, for all the other gospels. Hence, oral tradition under-lies written tradition (*testimonia*).

C. H. Dodd[1] has shown that the quotations from the Old Testament which appear in the New Testament exhibit all the main Christian doctrines. The apostles obviously had a common message which they proclaimed everywhere, and written sources were very probably reworded before reaching the form in which we now have them in the twentieth century.

Chronology

All scholars today agree that Mark is the first gospel to have been set down in writing. All Mark is in Matthew (except for a few verses), though not in the same order up to the end of Mt 13. Mark's Greek is very rough and Matthew, a converted scribe, tidies it up throughout in a schoolmasterly fashion. Matthew shows, too, a much later-Church situation than does Mark, and he clearly has his own theological purpose in his use of Mark.

Mark's gospel, as all agree, was written at the time of the fall of Jerusalem to the armies of Rome. Matthew is dated *c*80–85 AD, and Luke *c*85–90 AD; Matthew and Luke are independent of each other and of roughly the same date. John, as is proved by the Rylands papyrus,[2] dates to *c*90 AD. John Robinson[3] places all the gospels before 70 AD, on the grounds that there is nowhere to be found in them any reference to the destruction of the temple in that year.

Source Criticism

'Criticism' means scholarship, not pulling to pieces. Critical understanding is not the same as a naive grasp, but what is informed and reflective. The so-called 'source critics' unearthed what they called 'Q' (from the German *quelle*, a source), a written source containing the sayings not the deeds of Jesus. The critics were then able to discover that Matthew is a combination of Mark+Q+'M' – that is, 'M' being the material proper to Matthew and not found in the other gospels. Similarly, Luke is Mark+Q+L, the latter being Luke's own material.

So, Q is what is common to Matthew and Luke, but not in Mark: for example, Mt 11:25–7 equals Lk 10:21–2 (this being a standard method of reference in the Bible) but Mt 11:28–30 equals M. What is called *midrash* in Matthew is commentary (reflective meditation). Matthew is far longer than the other synoptic (overall view) gospels, John being a largely Christian meditation. Matthew is *usually* longer than Mark or Luke in *sayings,* as he is interested in Jesus as teacher and therefore cuts down on the narrative. Mark is often longer on narrative, more colourful, and it would be extraordinary if anyone, using the other, did it the other way round (*cf* the attitudes to family and disciples in Mt 12:46–50, Mk 3:31–5, Lk 8:19–21).

Form Criticism

The question put by scholars was: 'Can we get behind the period between the events and the first written words?' That is, back to the oral tradition. The latter was first in Aramaic, and the assumption behind the question is that the oral tradition would be 'more authentic' because not overlaid by 'faith' interpretations or embroidered, with stories growing in the telling. But is such an assumption correct? Are we dealing with oral tradition or *traditions*? No two people would give the same account of *any* event, or of any person. Might what appears in writing be an intentional correction of one oral tradition by another? And, anyway, is 'faith vision' *less* true or authentic? And does written tradition start after oral?

Whatever may be the case with such questions, the gospels circulated in separate units (*pericopae*), as may be seen from the way the synoptists shunt them around. The 'form critics' looked for patterns formed in these units; for example, stories, sayings, parables, and other very complicated names. R. Bultmann[4] on John found signs – sources (symbolic rather than historical miracles), revelatory discourses savouring of the Eastern Roman Empire and Gnostic writings.

The form critics were in danger of vicious circles and over-rigid patterns: 'What does not fit into my pattern must be a later addition', and so on. But they did have one important insight: that of the *sitz im leben* (life situation) of Jesus, of the Church, of the gospel. For example, 'Thou art Peter,' (*cf* Mt 16:13–23 and Jn 6:67–9 for Peter's confession).

Redaction Criticism

The phrase 'redaction criticism' covers the characteristic

theology and means editorial–approach–scholarship. Redaction critics are concerned with the characteristic theology of each of the authors of the gospels, editing his material, with little touches here and there to convey his emphasis, his point of view. For example, the handling of the disciples (*cf* Mk 8:32 and Mt 16:22, or Mk 9:30–2 and Mt 17:22–3).

Mark

'Marcus' is a common Latin name. Papias of Hierapolis (*c*120 AD) is quoted by Eusebius (third century) as writing that Mark was Peter's interpreter (translator into Greek) 'who wrote down accurately . . . all that he remembered of what the Lord had said and done.'

Who? When? Where?

In the *who*, *when*, and *where* of Mark's gospel, this observation by Papias has a good claim to historical accuracy. It is supported by 1 Pet 5:13: 'She [the Church] who is at Babylon [Rome] . . . sends you greetings and so does my son Mark.'

Though Mark's gospel is shorter than the other gospels, he mentions Peter more often (25 times); and Peter is very prominent (*cf* Mk 1:36, 14:37, and 16:7). Mark also combines an exceptional number of Latinisms (for example, Mk 12:42) and Aramaic formulae. As a Greek-speaking Jewish Christian from Jerusalem who understood Aramaic, he translated many Aramaic expressions (*cf* Mk 3:17, 5:41, 7:11, 15:22, 15:34, 36:45). He is usually identified with the John Mark of the Acts of the Apostles (*cf* Acts 12:12); so wrote the scholar, Martin Hengel:

> The Greek-speaking John Mark, whose house Peter visited first in the legend of Acts 12:12ff, after his liberation from prison, was presumably his companion and interpreter where that was necessary.[5]

It is thought by some scholars that Mk 13 illustrates that the destruction of Jerusalem (70 AD) had taken place, but

Hengel argues that it is woven out of material from the Old Testament and apocalyptic literature. Thus, the event has not yet taken place. Daniel's *abomination of desolation* has become a person in Mk 13:14 and there is widespread reference to the rumour that Nero would come to life again (he died in 68 AD), enthrone himself in Jerusalem, and then ravage the West. In a speech made by Jesus there is an aside to the reader (*cf* Mk 13:14) which means that the reference to 'Nero Redivivus' would be recognized. This dates the gospel precisely to the winter of 69/70 AD, when the civil war – as well as the Jewish war – was raging (*cf* Mk 13:7–8). The Christian community at Rome would have had a special reason to fear a return of Nero and is consequently warned of impending persecutions and defections (Mk 13:9–13). So, with the confirmation of 1 Pet 5:13, there is no reason to doubt that Mark's gospel was written in and for the Christian community in Rome.

Characteristics of Mark

Matthew is the 'gospel of the Church'; Mark has been neglected until comparatively recently. It is hard to see and hear Mark, he is full of vivid description. In Mark, Jesus is a craggy personality (*cf* Luke's Jesus) and prophets are not comfortable people. Mark is hard on the disciples and their 'stupidity'. One commentator has the theme of *insider* and *outsider* and thinks that even the disciples end up as outsiders.[6]

From Mk 8:31 onwards, Jesus concentrates more on the disciples than the crowds, though not exclusively. Mark is hard on Jesus' family also in a passage following on the Call and the naming of the Twelve (Mk 3:31–5=Mt 12:46–50=Lk 8:19–21).

In Mark, only Jesus proclaims God's 'kingdom'. The word in Aramaic more usually means the activity of reigning rather than the realm. The kingdom or kingship is not a body of doctrine but a 'mystery', that is a *secret* which Jesus himself embodies but reveals only to the disciples.

There is a strange verse about the parables (Mk 4:12). Surely it is the whole point of a parable that its lesson is immediately obvious to all and sundry; so, why should

Jesus *conceal* its point from the crowds? One answer may be that Mark is faced with a great problem: why, after all God's preparation over the centuries, did the Jews not believe in Jesus? Surely God must have meant them to do so? Mark puts forward the reasoning of this verse as his answer.

It is in Mark, too, that Jesus confronts the forces of evil: one example is that of the Gadarene swine (Mk 5:1–20). People pity the poor swine, but do not realize that a pig is abhorrent to a Jew; further, the sea was thought of as the deep terror whence all monsters arose to threaten men and women. So Jesus is sending the evil back to where it came from!

The story of the feeding of the 5,000 first appears in Mk 6 and is 'doubled' in Mk 8. One scholar wrote, 'If this is not a doublet then there are none in literature.'[7] But it isn't: the 5,000 represent the Jews and the 4,000 the gentiles, indicated by 12 and 7 baskets of fragments respectively.

Another writer, William Vanstone,[8] points out that from the time when Judas handed over[9] Jesus in the garden, Jesus, who through the gospel had been in charge, henceforth ceases to take the initiative. He simply has things done *to* him (*passion* means just that).

Luke

The first questions to ask about Luke are the same as in the case of Mark: *Who?*, *When?*, *Where?*

In Lk 1:1 and Acts 1:1 it is demonstrated that Luke is a historian after the manner of Thucydides, obtaining his material from reliable sources and recounting things accurately. Luke puts into the mouths of people such as Peter the sort of speech he considers appropriate to the occasion, as Thucydides did in the famous speech of Pericles about the island of Melos.

Tradition from Irenaeus (c180 AD) onwards has identified Luke with the 'beloved physician' (Col 4:14), and there is no reason to doubt this. As the passages in Acts, where Luke uses 'we' and not 'he' (Paul) show, Luke accompanied Paul on his travels and his gospel is obviously written for a Hellenistic church of the Pauline type. However, except that it is very hostile to Judaism, Luke's gospel and Acts show no awareness of the controversies with Judaism in which Paul was engaged; it may be that this issue was dead by Luke's time.

There are indications, too, that Luke was a doctor: in describing Jesus curing a fever (Lk 4:38), Luke uses an unusual medical term (*cf* Lk 5:12) and he omits the criticism of doctors found in other versions of the same incident (Lk 8:43); he again uses medical terms when describing cures for illnesses (Acts 28:7–10). Eusebius reports a tradition that Luke came from Antioch; indeed, Luke shows much knowledge of that church (*cf* Acts 11:19–26, 13:1–3, 15:1–5, 18:22, 22–35). Other suggestions are that Luke was a convert from paganism (Col 4:10–14).

Luke gives a detailed description of the destruction of Jerusalem (Lk 21:5ff), but this does not show that he was writing after that time (70 AD), as the material could have been drawn from traditional Old Testament and apocalyptic pictures. But he is after Mark, whom he uses, and his whole attitude is to dampen down eschatological expectation, so as to convey that the End is not so nigh, that the time of the Church means a long struggle and to encourage Christians to live with the Roman establishment. For example, he corrects the impression of Acts and Matthew that the fall of Jerusalem signalled the coming of the Kingdom. He does so by dividing the eschatological discourse between Lk 17 and Lk 20 (presence of the Kingdom) and Lk 21:20 (fall of Jerusalem).

There has been a tradition from Irenaeus onwards that Luke's gospel was composed in Greece, but it may still be for the church at Antioch.

Characteristics of Luke

Luke and Acts are certainly by the same author, as is shown not only by Acts 1:1, but also there is the same style prevailing, the same emphasis and the same parallels between the birth of Jesus (the Spirit and Mary) and the birth of the Church (Spirit and Mary).

There are three accounts of Paul's conversion (Acts 9:1–9, 22:3–21, 26:9–20) and they are not consistent with each other, as far as who saw or heard Jesus on the road to Damascus. Luke is writing history from various sources. He is a late author for this if for no other reason: Acts 1:8 ('to the end of the earth', by which he means Rome) reads like a table of contents (Jerusalem, Judaea, Samaria, and so finally to Rome).

There is a parallelism between Peter and Paul, Peter having roughly the first half of the book and Paul the rest. Throughout, there is an emphasis on the Spirit: at the conception of Jesus (Lk 1:35), at the start of the public ministry, and at the birth of the Church (Acts 1:2, 1:5, 1:8). There is also an emphasis on *women*, for example, Mary, the woman who was a sinner (Lk 7:36–50); the healing of a woman in the synagogue (Lk 13:10–17); and Martha and Mary (Lk 10:38–42; see also Jn 11:1 and 12:1–3).

Luke has much about the *marginalized*. For example: the Samaritans, who were the people who remained in Israel at the exile and kept to their religion as it was then (*cf* Jn 4) but were rejected by the Jews who returned from exile; the grateful one of the ten lepers who was a Samaritan (Lk 17:19): and there is, of course, the parable of the Good Samaritan.

Another theme is that of *universal salvation*, that is the gentiles are included in God's plan. Luke's is the *gentle* gospel, presenting a much softer picture of Jesus; the Prodigal Son and the Good Samaritan are examples, showing the Father's mercy. Luke omits elements unflattering to Peter, whereas Mark (speaking for Peter) brings out the stupidity of the disciples time and time again. Luke's is the *gospel of the poor* and shows much concern with wealth in the Hellenistic, well-off, churches. Matthew's beatitude reads: 'Blessed are the poor in spirit', but Luke's reads: 'Blessed . . . are the poor.' Other examples are those of the Unjust Steward (Lk 16:1–13), the Rich Man and Lazarus (Lk 16:19–31), and the Parable of the Fool (Lk 12:13–21). Luke also dampens down the pressing hope that the world is going to end any day with the Second Coming of Jesus. He is, therefore, all for making a go of living with the Romans (never the oppressors of the Jews, to whom they gave peace after years of foreign war) and is much kinder to Pilate than are other gospels.

Luke's gospel draws a threefold distinction between the time of the Old Testament, the time of Jesus, the time of the Church. And *journeys* are a constant feature: for example, around Galilee (Lk 4:15–9:50), but his topography is symbolic. Everything centres on Jerusalem: a lake is a place of evil (*cf* Gadarene swine); a mountain a place of revelation, with the crowds absent; a desert is where you pray; a plain is where you meet the people. Then there is the journey to Jerusalem itself (Lk 9:51–19:28), when Jesus says it *must* be that he would suffer for this in God's plan and will. The journey shows a set progress towards the Passion. Everything in Luke centres on Jerusalem where Jesus dies, rises, appears, and sends out the apostles.

Luke, in fact, shows ignorance of the real geography of Palestine, having Jesus pass south from Galilee *between* Samaria and Judea. He omits some events (for example, Mk 6:45–8 and 8:27) because it does not fit into his journey plan – a 'theological geography' – to have Jesus operating outside Jewish territory, for that is for the Church to do (the Gadarenes are obviously gentiles, across the northwest part of the lake).

Matthew

Who?

The question *who* rests largely on a false assumption of 'author'. Matthew is very clearly the product of a *church* with its own situation and emphasis. It very probably originates from Matthew the apostle (all lists have a Matthew), but it is very unlikely that the final version is due to a follower of Jesus (Matthew alone calls the tax collector 'Matthew', the rest having 'Levi').

When?

As to the *when*, the date is usually put at *c*80–85 AD and appears to be after the fall of Jerusalem (Mt 22:7; *cf* Lk 14:21–2), for Matthew uses Mark, including all but a few verses (*cf* the parable of the Marriage Feast, Mt 22:1–14). There seems to be confrontation with a revived Judaism (at Jamnia after the disaster of 70 AD). The break with Judaism is, however, by no means final, since the church at Jerusalem is being led by James, a hardliner on the law. Much hostility is shown to the Pharisees (the 'Separatists'), who were the leaders, rather than the people as a whole. There is a last, desperate attempt to appeal to the people over the heads of the leaders. The diatribe against the Pharisees (Mt 23) is mostly proper to Matthew.

Characteristics of Matthew

Throughout Matthew there are 'catchphrases' which both help the memory and mark the divisions in the sections (*cf* Mt 6:1–6, 7:28, 11:1). So the gospel was organized for teaching, preaching, liturgy. There is much more quotation of, or allusion to, the Old Testament than in Mark or Luke. A particular feature of Matthew are the *formula quotations* (*cf* Mt 4:14–16): here the passage brings out the *fulfilment* of scripture (that is, the Old Testament) in bringing to *fullness* the vision of history which pervades this gospel (*cf* Mt 13:52, 'old things and new'). There is a continual manipulation of the Old Testament texts according to what is called the '*pesher* method', which interprets the text in terms of what God meant by it; the result is a paraphrased translation.

For Matthew, Jesus is the fulfilment (fullness) of the Torah, both as God's true and final teacher and because his moral teaching is a recall to the chief inspirations and hopes of Israel, a recall from law to personal relationship (Sermon on the Mount). He pleads with the Jews to return to this spirit, and to see in Jesus and in the church a realization of their own destiny.

A mention of the church leads to the observation that the church of Matthew has very clear and distinct features of its own; it is up against a Judaism revived after the disaster of 70 AD, led by the Pharisees (since the Sadducees had lost all their power) and based on the new 'school' they had founded at Jamnia (modern Jabneh). Hence the hostility to the Pharisees, who were in fact pious and strictly law-abiding Jews keeping close to what God had taught them.

Matthew's gospel, as we have seen, is organized with care (many think it can be divided into five 'books', corresponding to the five books of the Pentateuch), and so set over against the law of Moses, with Jesus as a teacher to take the place of Moses. It has special material from a Jerusalem source (for example, the stories of what happened in Jerusalem after the death of Christ, and the 'Thou art Peter . . . ' passage, and so on). Peter may well have been the one who first preached the gospel in Rome, as Paul writes to converts in Rome who were not connected with his own missionary work.

John

Who?

To ask *who* is the wrong question, as we do not know. John's is the latest of the gospels, perhaps about 90 AD, inspired by a writer who is in charge of a local church. The original source is surely 'the beloved disciple', but we do not know who he is either, though the fact that the gospel never mentions John by name makes it almost certain that it was he.

The gospel originally ended with Jn 20 (*cf* the last verses in that chapter) and so the next chapter (Jn 21) is an addition; it is by another writer who uses words that never occur in the gospel. He is obviously concerned to contrast Peter and the beloved disciple.

When and Where?

The *when* and *where* lean toward an external tradition which says that the gospel was written at Ephesus, the capital of the Roman province of Asia and long since silted up and miles inland in modern Turkey. John Robinson[10] argues that the community started in Palestine (they are the 'Greeks' of Jn 12:20), are Jews who have come up for the feast but do not speak Aramaic, and that they then moved on to Asia Minor. Robinson stresses that the gospel never mentions gentiles and is wholly concerned with the inter-Jewish differences and that John was written against Palestinian Pharisaic Judaism (it is extremely hostile to the Jews and is perhaps aimed to convert the diaspora Jews of the city).

The Prologue

There is no infancy narrative in John. The testimony of John the Baptist is woven into the prologue. In the past, scholars argued for all kinds of sources of the prologue: weird Mandaen and Hermetic writings, and so on. It appears to be a hymn, probably pre-Christian, but Raymond Brown in his commentary on John,[11] shows that every phrase is traceable to the Wisdom literature of the Old Testament, so there is no need to look further. Logos is masculine, presumably chosen by John because Jesus was, but the words 'Spirit', 'Word', and 'Wisdom' are interchangeable, and as the passage is woven from the Wisdom literature, we should think of the wisdom of God being made man.

As the work is written in Greek, the word covers two ideas, the Jewish and the Greek: namely, the idea of the mind of God with its pattern for human life, and the Jewish idea that God is in charge – God created for the sake of Israel – and so this passage looks towards salvation. 'In the beginning', the opening words, evoke the fact that God is the source of life, not only a start in time. At various points, the gospel keeps marking off 'on the first day . . . the third day . . . ', and some scholars have seen in this a reference to the 'days' of creation in Genesis.

John is anti-docetic.[12] In other Christian tradition, Jesus is filled with the Spirit, both at his conception and baptism and at his exaltation (Acts 2:36). In John, he is divine in origin and descends (*cf* Jn 3:13 and 6:33). This gospel is so different because it is written to demonstrate the prologue, and in it Jesus is a divine figure throughout.

Characteristics of John

The *chief* Christology is that of the Son of Man – one from above who must go away/ascend. It is a characteristic of

John that words have double meanings: Nicodemus takes Jesus literally about being born 'again', whereas Jesus means 'from above'. Jesus is one whose work here anticipates his role in the judgment: he is the light of the world, judges/shows up/gives eternal life to all who believe in him. To see/believe/hear him is to have life and escape judgment.

The only events common to John and the synoptics between the baptism of Jesus and the Last Supper are the feeding of the 5,000 and the walking on the water, plus the cleansing of the temple at the start of Jesus' ministry. This gospel is certainly written for the Christian who knows the Jesus tradition: for example, Barabbas is not explained (Jn 18:40 and *cf* Mk 15:7). Bultmann, a very radical critic, holds that there were not any miracles[13] – the stories were added to make Jesus competitive with other religious leaders and miracle workers, such as Apollonius of Tyana; the speeches were in poetic vein, modelled on pagan literature.

Other opinion is that John has some material of his own, modelled on imaginative use of the synoptics. Lazarus (not in the synoptics) is crucial to the story of the death of Jesus; he is devised from the parable of the rich man and Lazarus in Luke: 'Even if one came back from the dead they would not believe,' (Lk 16:31), a passage proper to Luke.

John answers second level questions, such as: 'Who is Jesus?' Miracles are not powers but 'signs' of who Jesus is: in Jn 6:29–36, Jesus has worked the miracle of the 5,000 the evening before, and yet the Jews are still asking for a sign. Jesus, talking of the bread from heaven, says that *he* is the sign they are looking for. In John there is a running theme of seeing/believing (*cf* Jn 6:36 and especially Jn 9:35–41; see also, Jn 20:8 and 20:30–1).

The Samaritans, who rejected the David tradition and only accepted the Pentateuch of the Old Testament, are depicted in Jn 4 as having a whole village converted (without John there would hardly be the fact that Jesus ever went to Samaria) and perhaps this is the source of John's material?

The conflict with the synagogue is great and shows that the separation of Christianity from Judaism is now complete.

Another characteristic of John's gospel is the dualism of dark/light, and so on, as at Qumran. The 'Gnostic' language prevented the work from being accepted in the Church until the fourth century or thereabouts. I often think of John as an organist with three hands playing in three different registers – as in the Nicodemus story (Jn 4) where there is an ambiguity in the use of the phrase 'from above': poor Nicodemus thinks that Jesus means we have literally to be *born again*, whereas John means 'from above'. So, too, the passage where he is to be lifted up (Jn 3:14–15, 8:28, 12:31–2).

A further feature of John's gospel is the scenes which are 'on stage': for example, there are one-to-one encounters with Nicodemus, Pilate, and the Samaritan woman. John's church is not institutional (cause of its downfall), it knows of the Twelve but only uses *apostle* once (Jn 13:16), where it means 'messenger', as it does in all John.

The attitude to women in John's gospel is at least egalitarian; it is Matthew, not Peter, who confesses Jesus, and Mary Magdalen, not Peter (*cf* 1 Cor), who is the first to see the Lord.

There is an apparent fatalism, as with other evangelists, but it is likely that the ambiguities protect the carefully protected secret of the in-group.

Matthew's Infancy Narrative

Genealogy, Mt 1:1–17

The genealogies of both Matthew and Luke are literary compositions, and it is misguided to try and harmonize them.

Matthew gives Jesus' descent from Abraham via David, while Luke gives it from Adam. Matthew has three cycles of 14 generations, corresponding to the three periods of Israel's history, Abraham to David, Solomon to exile, and the post-exilic period. The arithmetic, 14=2x7 is a perfect number. The third group only has 14, if either Mary is counted or Jesus is counted (*cf* Mt 1:17). Jesus is the fulfilment of the promise to Abraham and of the covenant with David.

The Birth of Jesus, Mt 1:18–25

The virgin birth is indicated in Mt 1:16, and stated in Mt 1:18. It is not mentioned in the New Testament apart from the infancy narratives.

The Magi, Mt 2:1–12

The theological point of the story is that Jesus is the king Messiah of Old Testament expectation (*cf* Mt 2:2, where the Magi ask where the king of the Jews has been born). The story says three gifts were given, not that there were three Magi (who are Chaldean astrologers). There are political implications of the birth in that Jesus is rejected by the Jews but accepted by the gentiles.

The Flight into Egypt – Massacre and Return

These are stories exhibiting fulfilment of the Old Testament. Jesus is the true Israel, called out of Egypt as in the Exodus; the *whole* of Israel is summoned, since Rachel is mother of the northern kingdom as well as of Judah.

Luke's Infancy Narrative

Far more Semitic than the rest of the gospel, Luke's infancy narrative evokes the Semitism of the LXX.[14] Either Luke is consciously imitating the LXX in these stories, or he is using as sources a Greek version of Aramaic traditions – as he indeed says (Lk 1:1–4). And, it is only Luke who records the origins of John the Baptist.

The narrative consists of two diptychs: the annunciation and birth of John and of Jesus. Their purpose is to show the incomparable superiority of Jesus over John, and to proclaim the fulfiment of messianic expectation in Jesus, who is called Great, Holy, King, Light and Glory, Son of God, Saviour, and Christ the Lord.

One may note that in the presentation story it is not

required by the law that the first born should be presented in the temple. The event is important to Luke as 'accomplishing' the dedication of Samuel (*cf* Lk 1:22, 1:23, 1:57, 2:6, 2:21). Hence, Mary is in a priestly role, dedicating Jesus to his task (the fulfilment of Mal 3:1), saying:

> Behold, I send my messenger to prepare the way before me, and the Lord whom you seek will suddenly come to his temple; the messenger of the covenant in whom you delight, behold, he is coming, says the Lord of hosts.

So, Lk 1 and Lk 2 begin and end in the temple.

Finally, it may be noted that there is strong evidence of the influence on the Johannine circle of Luke's gospel.

The Passion Narratives

General Aspects

The Passion narratives are the only really continuous narrative in the gospels; indeed, Wrede's opinion is that a gospel is a story of the Passion preceded by a long introduction.[15]

The story is told dramatically and is in fact dramatized by the Church in Holy Week. It exists in all four gospels (and, apart from the Passion, John has only two or three incidents in common with the synoptics). It is thought by some opinion to have been put into shape first, before the public life which began with John the Baptist; this is possibly an inference from 1 Cor 15:3, where Paul recounts the tradition as it was originally delivered to him.

Matthew is very close to Mark, except that he has some vivid material of his own: the fate of Judas; the earthquake, with the dead appearing in the city; the dream of Pilate's wife – much of it like the heavenly phenomena of his infancy narrative. Luke differs from Mark more than elsewhere, and may have an independent source or sources, or may just be embellishing older tradition. He has the Jesus-Pilate-Herod episodes, not found in the other gospels, and perhaps had contact with Herod Antipas sources at Antioch (*cf* Acts 13:1), though he mixes up the different Herods.

John is quite different: Roman soldiers involved in the arrest; Annas; the dialogue with Pilate, with its 'enter' and 'exit' stage directions, as in the story of the Samaritan woman.

Gethsemane

In Mark and Matthew, Jesus prays three times for the cup to be taken away and shows great signs of distress. Some conflict is seen with the fact that he had predicted the Passion three times and had challenged the disciples: 'Can you drink the cup . . . ?' It is possible that Mark's account reflects persecution of the Church by Nero (probably instigated by Nero's mistress who was Jewish), and Mark is offering encouragement.

In Luke, the angel strengthens Jesus and *then* he enters his *agonia*, a technical term for an athlete gathering all his strength for the contest. Jesus' sweat is said to be *like* drops of blood, not a sweat of blood.

Luke plays down the weakness of the disciples in the supper and Gethsemane narratives: at the supper, 'You are those who have continued with me . . . ', not 'You will all fall away . . . '; to Peter, 'Satan will sift you, but I have prayed for you . . .', an assurance that Peter will come out on top; there is little or no separation from them in the garden ('a stone's throw'); and the disciples sleep 'through sorrow'.

In John, there is no prayer in the garden, agony, distress or sleeping disciples, but in Jn 12 when the Greeks came, 'Now is my soul troubled . . . ' (Jn 12:27-9); the prayer is answered by God/angel, and Jesus is very much in control throughout. Phrases of the Our Father are echoed: ' . . . thy will be done', ' . . . pray that you may not enter into temptation'; and 'Father, glorify thy name' (Jn 12:28).

Why the Execution?

In all their provinces, the Romans accepted the verdicts of

local courts but reserved to themselves sentence of execution (*ius gladii*). Pilate does not *condemn* Jesus in any gospel. It is clear that it was the chief priests and elders (that is, the Sanhedrin), not the Pharisees, who secured the death of Jesus. Jewish sources from very early times say that Jesus was put to death as a sorcerer (his miracles), who seduced the people away from the true worship of God. He certainly undermined the 'establishment' and cardinal points of the Torah and Jewish privilege. So he was *guilty*.

The charge brought to Pilate was that of threatening the temple, for there was his saying, 'Destroy this temple . . . ', which the gospels of both Matthew and Mark say was misused, and there was the cleansing of the temple; something like this was needed to persuade the Romans to execute.

If the Romans had thought Jesus was the leader of a revolt against Rome they would have put his followers to death too, yet the *titulus* was king of the Jews (Messiah). Pilate thought him harmless from a political point of view, perhaps slightly mad, and is mocking the messianic hopes of the people.

Pilate was a reasonable governor of a very tricky (and very minor) province and the Romans could never understand Jewish nationalistic and religious fervour combined – their own religion was just a social necessity. Pilate was probably too, a bit more anti–Semitic than most, as was Sejanus (the freedman favourite of Tiberius) who was influential in the appointment of governors of provinces. Sejanus fell from favour in 31 AD and Tiberius began his reign of terror. John's, 'You are no friend of Caesar . . . ', could be touching on a very raw nerve; Pilate's neck was on the block.

The Trial of Jesus by the Jews

The details of the trial of Jesus are somewhat suspect; for, where would the evidence of what took place come from – the disciples fled? The case against the legality of the trial does not stand up. We only have the *mishnah* version of the law, which is 200 years later and improved on the laws of the time.

Matthew, Mark and Luke all have the high priest pressing Jesus to say if he is the Messiah (he proclaimed the reign of God), and it was not blasphemous to claim to be the Messiah. Jesus answers in terms of the coming of the Son of Man, 'seated at the right hand of the Power', which is regarded as blasphemy, but Luke makes it depend on his saying he is the Son of God.

In John, no specific accusations are brought before Annas, and there is no account of the proceedings before Caiaphas: it is Pilate who asks Jesus, 'Are you king of the Jews?'

The Resurrection

The following points arise from study of the resurrection of Jesus Christ according to the New Testament.[16]

All four gospels tell of Jesus dying on the cross, and of his burial in a nearby tomb outside Jerusalem; but they vary in recounting the sequel.

The Sequel to Jesus' Burial

In the New Testament, there are a number of ways of referring to what happened after the burial of Jesus.

—The Christian hymn in Phil 2:5–11 recounts Jesus' exaltation to heaven, his adoration by all creation, and the new name 'Lord' given to him as he shares the throne (that is, power) of God. There is no reference to 'resurrection'. Jesus appears to be exalted straight from death on the cross.

—Another hymn is that in 1 Tim 3:16. Here Jesus' death is not mentioned, but after it he is vindicated by the Spirit, seen by angels, preached among the nations, believed in throughout the world, taken up in glory. No mention of resurrection.

—In Jn 12:32 (*cf* Jn 8:28 and 12:34) Jesus says: 'If I be lifted up from the earth, I will draw all to myself.' Being lifted up on the cross is seen as the beginning of the process of exaltation to glory.

—Jesus on the cross says to the thief: 'Today you shall be with me in paradise,' (Lk 23:43). Once more, the 'today'

implies a direct passage from death to glory.
—The same is implied in Lk 24:26: 'Was not the Messiah
bound to suffer all this, before entering his glory?' On
the evening of the day of resurrection, Jesus has entered
his glory without any reference to the ascension.
—None of these passages *deny* the resurrection.
—Paul, in giving versions of the primitive proclamation,
often refers to resurrection (*cf* Rom 4:25, 1 Cor 15:3–5, 1
Thess 1:10). See also Peter's proclamation on the day of
Pentecost (Acts 2:32–33).

The Empty Tomb

New Testament accounts of the risen Christ and the empty
tomb are numerous.

—All four gospels begin the sequel to the Passion with the
account of the empty tomb. But then they all go different
ways.
—Matthew develops a tradition answering objections
about the empty tomb (Mt 27:62–6 and 28:11–15). Guards
were posted after the tomb was sealed, to prevent the
body being stolen and a claim of resurrection made; the
guards were later bribed to say the disciples had stolen
the body during the night.
—In 1 Cor 15:3–5, Paul only implies the empty tomb without mentioning it: '. . . he died . . . he was buried . . . he
was raised on the third day . . . '
—Narratives about discovering the tomb empty may have
later elements, but there is no reason to doubt that the
discovery itself took place.
—Empty tomb stories always contain the proclamation
that he is risen, by a young man or by angel(s).

Accounts of the Appearances

New Testament accounts of the appearances of the risen
Christ include.

—Mk 16:1–8 is the end of Mark's gospel. Discovery of the
empty tomb by the women, Easter proclamation made to

them, charge given them to go and tell the disciples and Peter that Jesus precedes them to Galilee, where they will see him. No appearance is recorded.

—Mt 28:1–20 is the end of Matthew. Discovery of the empty tomb by women and message given to them, as in Mark. Then Jesus appears to the women in Jerusalem on their way back. Story of bribing of the guards. Appearance to the Eleven in Galilee, where Jesus commissions them.

—Lk 23:56 to 24:53 is the end of Luke's gospel, with five episodes:

(i) Discovery of empty tomb, Easter proclamation, charge given to the women – but to recall what Jesus told them in Galilee: so, no mention of an appearance in Galilee. The women report but the disciples do not believe. Peter visits the empty tomb.

(ii) Appearance to two disciples on road to Emmaus.

(iii) Appearance to the Eleven and those who were with them in Jerusalem.

(iv) Christ commissions them to be witnesses to him.

(v) Christ leads them out to Bethany and is carried off to heaven. Christ appears only in Jerusalem, or nearby. An appearance to Simon is reported (Lk 24:34).

—Jn 20:1–29 is the real end of the gospel. Mary Magdelene, Peter and the beloved disciple visit the empty tomb; Christ appears to Mary; then to the disciples in Jerusalem with Thomas absent; then to them with Thomas present a week later. All three appearances take place in Jerusalem. There is a reference to the ascension (Jn 20:17).

—Jn 21:1–23 is an appendix, recounting appearance at the Sea of Tiberias; then Christ commissions Peter to feed his flock, and the roles of Peter and the beloved disciple are contrasted.

The Meaning of Christ's Resurrection

There are various interpretations of the resurrection.

—Matthias is chosen to fill the place of Judas as 'a witness to the resurrection': not a witness to the event, but to the fact of Christ's being risen.

—No account of the resurrection happening in the New Testament (supplied later by the gospel of Peter) but there are reports (Mt 28:2) of how the stone was rolled back by the angel.

—Resurrection never depicted as a resuscitation, return to this life (*cf* Lazarus).

—Risen Christ does not live on earth, but appears and disappears. New Testament repeatedly implies that he appears from his glory in heaven.

—So the basic affirmation is that on his death he passed to the Father's glory and presence, whether this is called exaltation, resurrection or ascension.

—Resurrection belongs to primitive Palestinian proclamation, and is never presented as 'immortality of soul', a Greek hope not shared by Jews. Resurrection means resurrection of the bodily self (Dan 12:2).

—Luke alone tries to describe ascension. At Lk 24:50–3 he depicts it happening at Bethany on Easter Sunday, but in Acts 1:9–11 it occurs on the Mount of Olives forty days later. One must understand that the ascension was the last appearance to the followers of Jesus assembled as a group, a farewell. Henceforth, they would be aware of his presence only 'in the breaking of bread' (Lk 24:35), and 'in the promise of my Father' (Lk 24:49), that is, the Holy Spirit as explained in Acts 1:4–5.

—Luke uses the Old Testament round number, 40, to separate resurrection (Easter) and ascension, in preparation for the fiftieth (Pentecost) day.

We may conclude by observing that, while an empty tomb proves nothing, an occupied tomb would have made it impossible to proclaim the risenness of Jesus precisely in terms of *resurrection*. It is in the risenness of Jesus that we believe, and that is not a past historical event but an eternal or eschatological reality. So it cannot be proved or disproved by historical methods.

It is important to distinguish *appearances* ('I/We have seen the Lord'), attested by Paul and others, from *appearance stories*, which may well be later embellishments.

Ecclesiology

The Church in the New Testament

The Church has many titles in the New Testament: the 'redeemed community of the risen Jesus', the 'assembly' (*ekklesia*) – that is those called by him, hence the 'saints' which does not mean holy.

The Jewish idea of holiness is that people and things are so called because God has chosen them: so, Holy Land, holy temple, vestments, altar, and so on. They are a missionary community doing what Jesus did and told them to do (Mk 3:14), aware of the 'Church of God' as present in the Jerusalem Christian community and then in other communities, a unity because his community. They were not aware of any particular structures as instituted by Jesus. The various 'offices' which developed were as a result of charismatic gifts shared by all, and include some everyday tasks, such as administration: their teaching is the teaching of the apostles.

The Theology of the Church

It is hard to get back behind the theologies of particular writers. Certainly the first Christians called themselves 'the saints' (so in the greetings of Paul's letters).

Paul writes of the community at Rome as the 'wild olive' grafted onto the true, and drawing its strength thence (Rom 11:17); they are the free people of God's promise , by contrast to disbelieving Jews, true descendants of Sara (Gal 4:21–31), children of the Jerusalem from above, our mother.

This is in tension with the prediction of Rom 9:11. In the end, for Paul, a new people of God comprising Jew and gentile, standing on the old, takes the place of the old, resting on the new foundation of faith in Jesus Christ, the Israel of God (Gal 6:16), to whom is transferred the blessing promised to Abraham (Gal 3:14 and 6:16); the true progeny of Abraham (Rom 4:11–17), in contrast to Israel according to the flesh.

In Ephesians, the secret of Christ bringing unity, now revealed (Eph 3:4), brings in a new man (Eph 3:15) redeemed and sanctified (5:26), growing into the full measure of the plenitude of Christ (4:11–16). There is equality of Jew and gentile in the Church with one Lord one faith one baptism (*cf* 1 Cor 8:5, Gal 3:26 and 1 Cor 12:13), made one by the one bread (1 Cor 10:17). They are the temple of the Spirit (1 Cor 3:16, 2 Cor 6:16), an idea possibly taken over from late Judaism and Jesus' saying, 'I will build another temple not made with hands' (Mk 14:58). Above all they are the Body of Christ, and Paul has an extremely realistic body theology, for example, 'the Lord is *for* the body (1 Cor 6:13).

1 Peter and Hebrews

In 1 Peter the spiritual household of which Christians are living stones (1 Pet 2:4–10) is a holy priesthood to offer up spiritual sacrifices (1 Pet 2:5), of which Jesus is the cornerstone (1 Pet 2:4 and see also Eph 2:20). The people of God, 'called out of darkness, have gained salvation' (1 Pet 2:9–10), the flock of God are pilgrims (1 Pet 1:17) who are strangers in this world.

In Hebrews, the Son leads the way for pilgrims, as Moses through the desert, towards the sabbath rest, the heavenly Jerusalem and Christian worship fulfils all the Jewish feasts.

In Revelation, the Church fulfils Israel, all its titles and privileges: kings and priests (Rev 5:10).

It is the eschatological Israel with 144,000 signed (12,000

for each tribe) and they sing the song of Moses (Rev 15:3). The heavenly woman=Eve=the Church, which bore her offspring against the dragon.

Pastoral letters

One searches for the idea of the Church underlying the letters, which are much later than Paul. In 1 Tim 3:15, the Church is a holy institution, 'the house of God, the Church of the living God, the pillar and ground of truth': strong and firmly founded. There is no sense of growth, as in 1 Corinthians, 2 Corinthians and Ephesians. The community itself, not the apostles and prophets (Eph 2:20), is the foundation. The house appears to be fortified (*cf* the fortified settlement at Qumran); the 'truth' consists of belief in Christ and approved doctrines (1 Tim 1:19). There are instruction and formation (Tit 2:12, 2 Tim 2:24–5), offices and discipline. There is a comparison with a household in 1 Tim 3:5, but simply with the material house in 2 Tim 2:19, well furnished. There is no mystical or eschatological or charismatic dimension (clearly not by Paul), and apostolic doctrine has become a 'deposit' which Paul commits to Tim to preserve (1 Tim 6:20). The gospel is for all, but the stress is on maintenance and the civic virtues rather than on mission and deep religious spirit. The Spirit, conferred by laying on of hands, is somewhat institutionalized.

Johannine writings

The gospel and letters were long considered to present an individualistic and spiritualized Christianity (not improved by Bultmann's existentialist interpretation[1]): salvation of the individual and union with Son and Father, with worship in spirit and truth (Jn 4:23). But entry into eternal life is only through baptism into the orthodox community. The Spirit regenerates in baptism but life has to be lived with the love of others. The Spirit is only operative and fruitful in the community, an impression reinforced by the eucharistic passages.

There is the image of the flock Peter has to feed (Jn 21), and the prayer (Jn 17) is for the unity of the flock. Another image is of the vine, evoking the Old Testament theme of God's people: Christians are the true Israel, they are the temple, the body of the risen Lord (Jn 2:21); their worship, however, is in spirit and in truth (constancy) (Jn 4:23); unity is that the world may believe, so theirs is a missionary church.

Hierarchial in Structure

All power and authority in the Church rests in Christ (Mt 28:18) and Church officers serve his authority and mediate it as ambassadors. The strictly regulated ranks of authority of Judaism and Qumran are absent, but development came in that direction.

Mutual support is variously attested and taught. However exalted, the Church is exposed to diabolic onslaughts (Eph 6:11). The Church, struggling on earth, tastes the powers of the age to come (Heb 6:5), and has not entered the sabbath rest; it is the historic people of God's love, election and covenant.

Old Testament themes are especially combined in 1 Pet 2:9 and the people of the Church are now a purchased people. They are not a new people but the old people with a new covenant now expanded to include all peoples. Hence, there is tension with persisting Judaism, and continuity co-exists with discontinuity. But who are they? In Matthew, the Church is the sacrament, the effective embodiment of who belongs, but they are not coterminous with the people of God.

The idea of the building of the Holy Spirit brings out the eschatological nature of the Church. *You* are the temple of God (1 Cor 3:16), an active and transforming indwelling (2 Cor 3:16–18), which grows into a holy temple in the Lord (Eph 2:20). Replacing the temple the people are a living temple with priests offering spiritual sacrifices in the fruit-fulness of their lives.

Later Views

Tertullian, when a Montanist, took a charismatic view,[2] thinking the essential nature to be Spirit, composed exclu-sively of spiritual people. So Hippolytus, 'the holy society of those who live in righteousness'. The Alexandrian ten-dency was to look to the Church of the true Gnostic while not ignoring the hierarchial institution, a gathering of the elect, a city ruled by God, the city of God and the Body of Christ, but also finds tension between the ideal Church which is holy and spotless. By contrast, Cyprian deals almost legalistically with the invisible Church which is the seamless robe of Christ.[3] The episcopate is the God-given principle of unity and is one and indivisible.

At Vatican II, the constitution *Lumen Gentium* is inconsis-tent with its leading notion, the people of God, which should include all Christians. In the *Decree on Ecumenism* it uses the concept of the 'one Church of Christ', which 'sub-sists' in the Roman Catholic Church, but also exists in all Christian churches. Hence, imperfect communion but also unity on the historical plane. There is a substantial unity given by Christ, which human frailty does not break.

The demythologizing of the New Testament is necessary in order to be faithful to the New Testament message and faith and one must strip off the pictorial world view to get at the message, the view of Jesus' time and of himself and his disciples. In doing so it is important to distinguish the certainty of the future of God's reign and kingdom and the conviction of imminence, especially as Jesus' resurrection was understood as the beginning of the resurrection of all, and so the reign was seen as present and active in Christian history, a pledge or first fruits of the future consummation. But it is important not to carry demythologizing through to de-eschatologizing, so that there is merely a meaningful present and no future fulfilment which is to empty out the hope that is an essential part of the New Testament message. This is the tenor of Bultmann's conversion of the message into the present decision of faith.[4]

True Christian eschatology holds at once to faith in the meaning of the present, indeed the meaning of man's historical and bodily present, which is where God works his salvation and not merely that of his spirit. The present is hastening towards a goal, that of finding meaning in its darkness, in its suffering from approaching Christ's light; the assured future is a realization of the imperfect present, and so depends on it. But the future also determines the present.

Man's assured hope, his decision of faith, is not just a consolation; not just a reason for turning away from the present, but for changing it. The word 'kingdom' usually means kingship, not a realm but a reign, but there can be no ruling without a people ruled, a people and not a territory or constitution. Neither Christian society nor the Church is God's kingdom. In reaction against over–identifications, theologians have separated them too completely.

Catholic triumphalism has led to Protestant depreciation of the Church as merely human, sinful: an absent Christ speaks his word through the Church and so on. Lesslie Newbigin is an excellent representative of this stance: Christ reigns, but in heaven, his reigning fleetingly appears on earth, in our history; the Church lives in the time of Jesus' conquest of death and before the manifestation of his death (in the future).

> The character of this time is given to it by the character of the earthly ministry of Jesus. It is marked by suffering and by the presence of the signs of the kingdom.[5]

The Church lives in hope of God's bringing in the kingdom and the coming of the kingdom is wholly God's work; it does not grow from within history, it is an irruption from outside.

Gerhard Lohfink, in his farewell address on resigning the chair of New Testament Studies at the Catholic faculty of

Tübingen University, wrote of the time of the kingdom that, current exegesis agrees, the present-future tension in Jesus' teaching should not be resolved, but nevertheless plays down the *presence* of the kingdom.[6] Everyone in Jesus' time believed God would establish his kingly rule in the future. What is unique about Jesus is that he proclaimed its presence, it had arrived (Lk 11:20). As to agents of the kingdom, men pray but can do nothing to bring it in. Obviously, the establishing of the kingdom is wholly God's work, but it is wholly man's action at the same time. God wholly gives but we do not wholly receive or respond.

A Charismatic Community

In Paul's letters the Church is depicted as a charismatic community rather than a hierarchically structured one, a Church in which office and leadership are included among the gifts which all have. This picture is needed in the Church at all times to balance and qualify tendencies towards absorption and legalism, and to ensure the full participation of all. It is the Spirit who maintains unity, not the authority of office, both unity in belief and in cooperation, mutual service and, in a word, in 'love' which is the greatest charisma of all.

The Church has at all times been menaced by enthusiasm, the privatising of the Spirit by a small group claiming esoteric knowledge that goes beyond the revelation of Jesus in the Church. Paul had to contend with this at Corinth. The second century saw Montanism and various other forms of Gnosticism and so on to Joachim of Flora and other mediaeval enthusiasts, not to be confused with Anabaptists, Quakers and the like. Enthusiasts have turned to John rather than Paul (the Paraclete leading into all truth) with the implication that this is not given to the Church.

So enthusiasm threatenes the charismatic community on the one side and clericalism on the other.

The sacramental model clarifies the relation of the

Church to the world. The Church is the community in which God's offer of grace to all is proclaimed, the visible sacrament of the invisible grace. This model can express both what is meant by the people of God and communion models, as well as tying together Christology, ecclesiology, and sacramental theology. It can be an over–introverted model but does not have to be.

Models of the Church[7]

The Church as Herald

This model makes 'word' primary and 'sacrament' secondary. It is more extrovert with less stress on personal relations.

It sees the Church gathered and formed by the word and commissioned to proclaim it, and is not responsible for whether or not the people respond. Karl Barth[8] saw the Church as constituted by the word being proclaimed and faithfully heard; it is an *event*. The fault of Catholicism and Modernism is to see the Church as proclaiming itself, pointing to itself as proclaiming what it contains, whereas the Church should be a herald of Christ's lordship.

In this model the bond of communion is faith, understood as a response to the gospel of Christ, and the sacraments are a dramatization of proclamation and response. The preaching is itself an eschatological event, the word of God on the lips of the preacher is impregnated with the power of God himself, and an eschatological event. The word saves those who believe in it.

The strengths of this position are the biblical basis in the prophets and Paul and a readiness for repentance and reform. Catholic criticism says the Word has been made flesh, whereas here in the extreme versions the Word has been made word! Further, the Church dissolves into a series of disconnected happenings and there is a too exclusive stress on witness to the exclusion of other actions, such as care for others.

The Church as Servant

In previous models of the Church, the stress has been on the Church seen as acting on this world. God comes to the world through the Church and *vice versa*. The text of Vatican II's *Lumen Gentium* reads like a rebuttal of Pius XII's, *Darkness Over the Earth* (published in 1939)[9], for the Church must see itself as part of the human family, sharing its concerns.

Teilhard de Chardin was a forerunner of servant ecclesiology; for him, the Church is the main focal point for the energies of love in the world. There is a tendency in modern ecclesiology to see the Church's task as, not primarily of proclaiming or spreading itself, but of discerning and serving God's presence in the world; of being of help to all in need.

The advantage of the model is to prevent introversion and to develop Christ's kingdom on earth, but it has no direct biblical foundation or basis in tradition. Neither Christ nor the Christian is, strictly, the world's servant; nor did the Church formerly think it had a mandate to change existing social institutions. That it can only fulfil its God-given mission by doing so is the modern insight; not by the individualistic and supernaturalist view of salvation the Church has so often pursued. And there is danger of leaving Jesus out of sight, at least until liberation theology.

The Church as Communion[10]

Any society has an ideology, a consensus about its nature and aims through which it achieves its identity. Counter-reformation theology prevailed until Vatican II, when it was seen to be no longer relevant to today's questions and when the biblical, liturgical, and ecumenical movements had eroded it. Today, the Church seeks to discover itself as communion.

The people of Israel had a sense of corporate identity and destiny, deriving from their relationship with God and giving their history the special purpose of being the vehicle for God's plans for all mankind. Corporate identity comes to expression in figures of the suffering servant of Isaiah and points to a single individual who will fulfil Israel's role in the plan of God, and to God's plan to bring success out of failure. After this prophetic image comes the apocalyptic image, the Son of Man, a corporate personality who will achieve Israel's task of bringing all peoples under God's reign. These are the primordial themes out of which eccelsiologies grow, and the Church sees Jesus as fulfilling them.

Paul in particular develops the idea of the Church as having corporate identity with Christ. The apostolic community shares in the Lord's fulfilment of Israel's destiny through baptism and the Eucharist. In Romans and 1 Corinthians, the Church is the individual bodily person of the risen Christ and the community are members of his body, not just a collective unity deriving from Christ. It is the agency of the Spirit through the sacraments which brings about this corporate union. In the later letters, Colossians and Ephesians, the lordship of Christ over principalities and powers leads to headship and this merges with the 'body-figure', which develops in patristic times into that of the 'whole Christ'.

Election is another Old Testament theme taken over by the Church, but election is for others and not for exclusive privileges (cf Is 2:2–4, 19:21-5, and 42:6); post-exilic and Pharisaic Judaism lost sight of this and became exclusivist. Jesus recalled Israel to universalism, stressing that Israel's election is for others (Mt 8:11) and Peter and Paul extended the Church's mission to gentiles. Luke is, of course, enthusiastic about universalism.

The patristic centuries by and large preserved the sense of the Church as an undifferentiated mystery, unanalysed, as the effective sign of God's plan for the whole of humanity – see especially, de Lubac's *Catholicism*[11] and *The Church, Paradox and Mystery*.[12] It was the Middle Ages which became exclusivist, and this goes together with institutional emphasis. Western civilization grew under the tutelage of the Church after the dissolution of the Roman Empire, hence the Church was the horizon of all society, while secular institutions grew in vigour and independence. The

Church was preoccupied with defining its relation to the State and the secular, hence thought about the Church was largely the preserve of canonists (ecclesiology is the invention of the twentieth century). Bellarmine defined the Church entirely in terms of its visible aspects as a 'perfect society'. The result is constitutional theory, not ecclesiology.

The rediscovery of the patristic heritage led by degrees to the recapturing of the mystery aspects of the Church. Today the category of sacrament is much favoured as combining the visible and faith aspects, but the Church is first and foremost a human community of people who follow Jesus and have a very personal relation to him. 'Sacrament' is a second order concept, not only technical and removed from ordinary understanding, but in danger of becoming abstract and obscuring the basic personal reality.

The Church is a community, not planned and organized by humans for human aims, but called into being by God. It is the community which is united to the spirit-body-self of the risen Lord, one in which a 'permanent presence of Jesus Christ in space and time is given to the world'.[13]

To call the Church 'communion' is to say that it is this community, but communion also means sharing, so the word further indicates that the community of the Church shares in the life of God by the gift of his Spirit. Hence it also shares in the chief expressions of God's saving works for men, the scriptures and sacraments. The word communion, then, reveals the Trinitarian structure of the Church (promised in Jn 17:22–3), for the Church is a continuation of the missions of Son and Spirit, and its institutional aspects exhibit the mission of the Son. Charismatic aspects are the life of the institutional ones, so the two together constitute sacrament.

It is necessary to stress this Trinitarian structure to avoid over-identification of the Church with institutional aspects and to avoid the opposite mistake of regarding God's work as exclusively spiritual and interior, and all institutional aspects as merely man-made.

New Testament Christology

Acts

In Acts there is a series of kerygmatic speeches by Peter and Paul (Acts 2:14–41, 3:12–26, 4:8–12, 5:19–32, 10:34–43). Jesus 'is a man pointed out to you by God by the miraculous signs he worked in Him' (Acts 2:14–22), ' . . . delivered up and crucified by the deliberate plan and foreknowledge of God' (Acts 2:14–23), ' . . . raised by God from the dead; as it was not possible for him to be held fast by death' (Acts 2:14–24), because David had foretold his resurrection (Ps 16:8–11). He is exalted at the right hand of God and has received the promised Holy Spirit from the Father and 'has poured him out on us' (Acts 2:14–33). 'God has made him Lord and Christ (Acts 2:14–36), so repent and be baptized in his name of forgiveness of your sins, and you will receive the gift of the Spirit' (Acts 2:14–38).

Here we have a characteristic functional approach – for sitting on the right hand and the power to dispense the Spirit are functions of God but set in an adoptionist framework: he receives the Spirit when exalted, and only then becomes Lord and Christ, so not in his lifetime.

In these speeches crucifixion is not seen as having saving power, the cross was simply a disaster for the disciples whose faith starts from the resurrection.

In Acts, the God of Abraham 'glorified his servant Jesus whom you betrayed and denied. You denied the holy and righteous one' (Acts 3:14) and 'put to death the leader to life' (Acts 3:15). In prophetic terms further verses characterize Jesus as God's Messiah: 'leader to life' probably means author of the way to salvation; he is said (Acts 3:22–3) to be the prophet such as Moses foretold in Deut 18:15. There is no evidence of any 'prophetic messianism' in Jewish literature, for the prophet expected and the Messiah are distinct figures. The link seems to be a Christian insight redefining 'Messiah' in terms of prophet, and there is less attribution to the risen Jesus of divine functions than in Acts 2.

Acts 4:12 before the Sanhedrin simply asserts that Jesus is the one and only saviour, the meaning of 'Jesus' (which is the reason why 'saviour' did not become a title) and repeats (Acts 5:31) 'exalted at his right hand as leader and saviour'.

In Acts 10, God anointed him with the Spirit and power to heal (Acts 10:34–8). 'He told us who ate and drank with him after his resurrection to proclaim that he is commissioned by God to be judge of living and dead'(Acts 10:41–2) and ' . . . there is forgiveness of sin for all who believe in him' (Acts 10:43).

In Acts 13, Jesus is the saviour whom God promised to David from his posterity (Acts 13:16–23), and he was raised from the dead following the promise to David (Acts 13:32–7).

As some of the language in Romans is not Pauline and the Christology is less developed than is his, Rom 1:3–4 is probably a pre-Pauline credal formula. There is an adoptionist and functional viewpoint; what Jesus was by birth is contrasted with what he became by the Spirit in his resurrection.

The Philippian Hymn

Here Paul is using an already existing hymn (Phil 2:6–11), possibly modifying it slightly. It is an example of 'homology', a proclamation of Christ with his titles as opposed to a creed professing faith in what he has done. Whereas Acts and Romans have a two-stage Christology, this hymn clearly envisages the pre-existence of Christ in some way, and has three stages:

(i) 'He was in the form of God', this is not a platonic form but an appearance.

(ii) 'He did not think equality with God as something to be grasped', but rather 'emptied himself' (source of kenotic theologies); in the context this means 'of the status or external glory of God', and the perspective is functional. 'Taking the appearance of a slave and appearing in the likeness of men' is not a reference to the Servant theme. The human state is subject to the demonic powers that rule this world (1 Cor 2:6–8), of which the last is death (1 Cor 15:24–6). It is over these that he becomes lord (*cf* Rom 8:3 for the 'likeness of sinful flesh');

(iii) 'He humbled himself becoming obedient unto death, even death on a cross'. Vawter[1] thinks Paul added the last phrase to the hymn to give it his own characteristic soteriology – that is, the cross is seen as salvific.

It could simply mean that Christ submitted himself to incurring death just by becoming man, and God's exaltation of him is the salvific event.

Those who think there is an allusion to the suffering Servant consider that 'humbled' echoes Is 53:7–8. The contrast could be with the disobedient self-exaltation of Adam. 'Wherefore God highly exalted him', balances 'emptied . . . humbled'.

There is no direct reference to the resurrection, which indicates that it is non-Pauline: the Greek word for 'highly exalted' is from John's usage.

The Name denotes power, as a result of which he is Kyrios with power surpassing that of all heavenly beings (*cf* 1 Pet 3:22; Heb 1:4; and Eph 1:20–3). This theme always recalls Ps 110:1, even when it does not quote it, and the picture is of Christ seated on the throne of God, sharing his power and pouring it out on us (note that the Name is not Jesus, but Lord).

The hymn quotes Is 45:23, and therefore transfers to Christ Kyrios the worship there given to God. 'Jesus Christ is Lord' is the earliest creed (*cf* 1 Cor 12:3 and Rom 10:9). The essential idea is functional: by his conquest of death

Christ has been given by God power over all the demonic forces that assail mankind.

Wisdom

Old Testament Background

The Wisdom literature of the Old Testament is a collection of wise saws, in which the term 'wisdom' was applied to man before its use for God.

The sayings summarize experience of life and constitute a genre of literature widespread in the Middle East, especially Alexandria (Egyptian influence). The transition of ideas is: there is an orderly pattern in nature and it is both morally wise and pragmatically sensible to follow it; God is the author of the order in the world; wisdom is God's plan, an attribute of his creative activity (*cf* Ps 104:24; Job 38:37; and Prov 3:19).

For Sirach, wisdom originates from God, but is identified with the word from God's mouth and with the law (Sir 24:3–23). God created wisdom before all else (Sir 24:9), while in Proverbs there is a wisdom about life not contained in the Torah. The author of the book of Wisdom meditates on the Old Testament and reflects on the personification of wisdom (Prov 1:8–9) and identifies wisdom with the Spirit of the Lord.

So, in the later literature, wisdom is no longer a creature, nor a separate Person, but a literary personification of one of God's attributes. The mysterious transcendence and inaccessibility of wisdom is stressed (Job 28 and 38, and Sir 1:1–10). Yet the whole process of theologizing wisdom is concerned with God's self-communication with men.

In the New Testament (1 Cor 1:18–24, 2:6–16 and 2 Cor 4:4–6), Paul is reacting against a tendency that later became Gnosticism, *viz* that salvation comes through knowledge rather than faith. It is Christ who is our saving wisdom, and a crucified Christ at that: God has made him our wisdom (1 Cor 1:30). So interpretation of Christ in terms of wisdom is early, just as is understanding of him as power (Phil 2).

In Romans there is a hymn to God's wisdom as revealed in his plan of salvation (Rom 11:33–6, *cf* 1 Cor 2:7–10). In Colossians the hymn starts with a salvation strophe (Col 1:18–20), preceded by a creation strophe (Col 1:15–17). A cosmic Christology has developed: the primacy of Christ in creation is the ground for his primacy in salvation, but only through the resurrection is the Redeemer thought to be first in all things; this Christology is not one of a timeless ontology but is dependent on the action of God in history. It is the incarnate Jesus who is said to be 'image' and 'firstborn' (*cf* the 'form' of God in Phil 2, who is said to be 'image' and 'firstborn').

Wisdom is a creature in the earlier wisdom literature (later the divine 'idea' or plan for all creation, the personified power of God) and stresses (Col 1:15) that all angelic powers are created, wherever he has lordship. The hymn probably meant the cosmos by 'the body', and the Pauline editor has substituted 'the Church'. As he is the firstborn in creation, so he is firstborn among the dead (Col 1:15–18). (For the fullness of God dwelling in Christ, see Col 2:9 and also Eph 3:16–19 and 4:10.) This is not metaphysical, but means the fullness of the divine saving power.

It is left somewhat ambiguous whether the hymn in its present form, and in its context in Colossians, refers to the pre-existent one (as Phil 2 clearly does), or the stress is on the risen Lord and his reconciliation, but the idea of pre-existence is implicit in the attribution to him of wisdom themes.

In Heb 1:2–4 the same thought pattern is exhibited; and these verses are also thought to be a hymn fragment. The outflashing of Christ's glory and the imprint of his being (image of a seal in wax) are virtually a paraphrase of Wis 7:26 whence the outflashing comes. Heb 2:15–18 spells out the idea of Christ 'for a short time less than the angels' as the emptying of the pre-existent one, who becomes lord of all powers.

John's prologue about the Logos obviously chooses the

word because Jesus is male, the ideas word-spirit-wisdom being equivalent. It is clear from the rest of John's gospel that his Christology is of a divine saviour who came down to earth to bring all up to God. He has adapted the hymn to this purpose. The 'fullness', as in Colossians, is that of the divine saving power. There seems nothing in the text to suggest that John is thinking of a *distinct* personal being: it is simply a personification of wisdom.

Messiah

Examination of the gospel evidence shows that Jesus did not claim to be the Messiah, and that when others pressed the title on him he avoided it. Yet we have the odd facts: that believers felt impelled to give him the title from the earliest stage, but to reinterpret it in the process; and yet very soon it became empty of content, a mere proper name in Paul, the commonest of all, by which believers came themselves to be known. Why? Because he was crucified under this title, king of the Jews, and because he preached the kingship of God.

The Messiah, however, is not an Old Testament name, for many kings, prophets, and the like, were called God's anointed because they had a special mission from him, Cyrus in Isaiah is an example (Is 45:1). One strain of Old Testament thinking is *royal messianism* but there persists a contrary strain, hostile to the kingship as a betrayal of God's rule; the oracle of Nathan (2 Sam 7:12–16) evidences the idea that the king is chosen by God as ruler of his people and the idea is much blown up in the royal psalms, composed for the coronation or anniversary of a king of Judah (*cf* Ps 2, 72 and 110). In the period of bad kings, Isaiah initiates the idea of a future descendant of David who will fulfil the ideal king-saviour role (Is 7:14–17 and 9:1–7; see also Mic 5:1–6), with a new David coming from Bethlehem, texts widely applied to Christ in the New Testament. There is later, in Jeremiah, sporadic mention (Jer 23:5, 30:9, and 30:21; see also Ezek 17:22). This kingly figure is a real future king and that the idea persisted is clear from its flowering in intertestamental literature, but there is little post-exilic biblical evidence available (*cf* Zech 9:9 and Hag 2:20–3).

The Hebrew Old Testament does not speak of the 'kingdom of God' (the phrase appears only in Wis 10:10) or of the 'messianic kingdom', but the expectation of a coming kingdom of God on earth, in which holiness and justness will prevail, depends on the hoped-for Son of David. In Isaiah, the kingdom is universalist and includes the gentiles (Is 42:6, 49:6); but universalism fades after the exile. The idea is to some extent spiritualized but remains a nationalist ambition.

'The Messiah' is a figure of Jewish apocalyptic. There are two main messianic figures, the Davidic and the priestly (hopes raised by the Hasmoneans, *c*BC 134). The Messiah is sometimes a heavenly and eschatological figure, sometimes this-worldly, sometimes a religious leader, sometimes a war hero.

The Messiah has a secondary role in apocalyptic literature, which turns on the whole to other-worldly and eschatological visions.

In the time of Jesus many, but not all, Jews expected the Messiah, for this was part of the Pharisaic creed, which accounts for Jesus' resistance, but the word covered a mixture of ideas and patterns, not a clear picture.

The Qumran community awaited the coming of 'the Messiahs of Aaron and Israel'; the expected prophet was a distinct figure, and could be either the prophet, like the Moses of Deut 18:15, or the returning Elijah of Mal 3:23 – or both run into one.

Jesus and the title 'Messiah'

The matter is complicated by the fact that the gospel accounts already exhibit editorial modification in the interests of the evangelists' theology. In Mk 14:61–4, Jesus before the high priest answers with an unqualified 'I am', but Mark has now made clear his view that it is only as suffering servant that Jesus is Messiah, so the title is now acceptable.

In Mt 26:63–4 and Lk 22:67–72, the answer is modified and seems the avoidance of a direct answer. Further, in all three accounts Jesus goes on to deflect attention from Messiah to the Son of Man passage from Dan 7:13; it is the latter which is the centrepiece of the narrative and it is this which constitutes blasphemy and not any claim to be the Messiah.

Before Pilate, who translates Messiah as 'King of the Jews', Jesus replied 'So you say', in all three accounts (Mk 15:2; Mt 27:11–12; and Lk 23:3–4). In Luke, Pilate goes on to say, 'I find no cause in him', so he did not take Jesus' answer as political. The dialogue on kingship in Jn 18:33–8 confirms the impression that Jesus' answer and Pilate's question are in different keys. In the narratives of the Caesarea Philippi incident (Mk 8:27), does Jesus accept Peter's 'You are the Messiah'? In all three accounts there is a transition to prediction of the Passion, and the disciples are forbidden to tell anyone Jesus is the Messiah. Peter's idea of the Messiah is a temptation in Mark-Matthew – it was Satan in the temptations in the desert who tempted Jesus to declare himself Son of God.

From all this scholars conclude that Christian reflection, which had decided Jesus was the Messiah in a new sense, is handling tradition in which Jesus disclaimed the title.

The Early Church hails Jesus as Messiah

Jesus preached the kingdom, he was crucified under the title 'INRI'. The royal messianic passages are among the earliest *testimonia* of the New Testament. In Acts 2 he became Lord and Messiah in his resurrection, and in Acts 3:20 'Christ' seems to be a fully eschatological title reserved for the end time. In Acts 3 Jesus' life work is characterized by servant and prophet – a Moses figure who will come again. The linking of servant and prophet with the title Messiah is a wholly Christian creation. The nearest parallel is the Samaritan Taheb (restorer) who was a looked-for teacher. Paul once or twice (*cf* 1 Cor 1:23) uses Christ as a title, and then to insist that we preach 'a crucified Messiah', but otherwise as a surname empty of content (the Messiah tradition would be meaningless to a Greek).

Son of Man

This is a minefield. In Aramaic, the word for 'man' denotes mankind. Son of Man is an idiomatic expression for mankind or a single individual man (*cf* son of perdition, and so on). In Psalms (Ps 8:4, 80:17, and 144:3) and in Ezekiel, where God addresses him throughout as Son of Man, it has the religious sense of 'man before God', mere man.

In Daniel the 'Son of Man' (Dan 7:13) carries primarily, and probably exclusively, a corporate sense (*cf* the corporate sense of 'servant') and depicts the collapse of four kingdoms and their rulers (Babylonians, Medes, Persians, and Greeks under Antiochus IV) symbolized by beasts. The man-figure in this passage, human as opposed to the beasts, denotes Israel (as is clear from Dan 7:18), 'the people of the saints of the most high'. So Daniel depicts the coming of the kingdom as the dominion of the true and faithful Israel. This is nationalistic, but not merely so; the effective kingship of God on earth through his people is foretold.

There is no indication that Daniel is thinking of any particular ruler of this final kingdom. In intertestamental literature no connection is made between Son of Man and Messiah: indeed, the ideas represent opposite poles of the tension in apocalyptic between the eschatological figure and the hoped for earthly ruler. Nor is 'Son of Man' treated as an individual, as opposed to a symbol for Israel, till a date so late that it is doubtful if there could be influence from this source[2] on Christian writers: the influence may be the other way.

Son of Man may be a Jewish version of an idea pervasive in the Hellenic world, and taking many forms, that of the 'heavenly man'. It was known to Paul (1 Cor 15:45–50) and helped his comparison of the two corporate personalities, Adam and Christ. Of specific Redeemer myths (the heavenly man descending into the world to rescue mankind) we only have evidence later than the New Testament, but the idea permeated the atmosphere breathed by Jewish apocalyptic, in which the Son of Man imagery took place.

To the time of Jesus, 'Son of Man' remained a symbol of the coming reign of God among men, mediated by Israel.

Use in the New Testament

The peculiarities of the title Son of Man are that only in the New Testament is the expression found: that, except for Acts 7:56 (on the lips of Stephen), it is found only in the gospels and nowhere as part of the teaching about Jesus; that in the gospels it is found only on the lips of Jesus and no one calls him Son of Man. Further, it is a Semitic expression and heavily tied to the centrality of Israel in God's designs. Perhaps this is why it was dropped. Yet it plays a central part in John, where it is the chief title, so it developed in the gospel tradition but was not used outside it.

At first reading the gospels suggest that it was the title Jesus preferred for himself; that he substituted Son of Man when Messiah was pressed upon him; in that case he was the first to introduce reference to an individual in place of the corporate sense of the phrase. He proclaimed that the Jewish aspiration, that God's kingdom would be made manifest on earth, was fulfilled in himself. Further, he made the connection, not suggested elsewhere, between Son of Man and suffering servant (itself both a corporate and individual image), a very paradoxical identification in view of the triumphal nature of the Son of Man figure: the Son of Man would bring in God's reign through suffering, for God would vindicate him.

However, scholars do not think the Son of Man Christology, at least as it is in the gospels, goes back to Jesus. The most critical view is that the whole complex of Son of Man sayings was first applied to Jesus by the early Church in the light of the resurrection.

Scholars have pointed out, too, that there are three groups of Son of Man sayings:

(i) Those in which Jesus refers to a future Son of Man com-
    ing as eschatological judge (Mk 13:26 and parallels),
    which clearly refer to Dan 7:13, but there is nothing to
    indicate that Jesus is referring to himself (*cf* the contrast
    between Jesus and the Q-saying in Lk 12:8: 'I tell you,
    whoever acknowledges me before men, the Son of Man
    will acknowledge him before the angels of God.').

(ii) Those in which Jesus identifies himself as a present Son
    of Man in his ministry. For example, the Q-saying in Mt
    8:20, Lk 9:58 and Mt 11:19=Lk 7:34; Mk 2:10 'the Son of
    Man has authority on earth to forgive sins'; Mk 2:28
    'the Son of Man is lord of the sabbath'.

(iii)Those in which Jesus speaks of himself as suffering and
    dying: the Passion predictions (Mk 8:31 and parallels).
    One may readily concede that these predictions do not
    go back to Jesus and hence that he did not identify Son
    of man and suffering servant.

Against this extreme position, however, one may argue
that it is extremely improbable that the early Church
worked out a complex interpretation of the risen Christ as
Son of Man, which was then found unhelpful for teaching,
if there was no foundation for it in the sayings of Jesus. A
merely deprecatory use of the title by Jesus to cover the second group of sayings is not plausible: such a use is not
attested elsewhere; and the sayings include those asserting
authority and power. Why should it be only on the lips of
Jesus, with such complex associations of ideas, if it never
was on his lips or only in reference to another Son of Man?
Further, there are many sayings in Q which have a claim to
be authentic: Mt 8:20=Lk 9:58; Mt 11:19=Lk 7:34; perhaps
the first half of Mk 10:45, not the second; Mt 12:32; Lk 6:22,
11:30, and 19:10. Some indicate a servant of God whose lot
is to undergo rejection in fulfilment of a prophetic mission.
Again, even without predicting his resurrection, Jesus
could well have seen himself in terms of Wisdom, as
prophetic servant of God due to be rejected by men but vindicated by God (Wis 2:12–20, 4:10–17, and 5:1–5).

For whatever reason, the title developed in the gospels

was dropped, though its content reappears elsewhere, partially in Paul's use of the second Adam, but mostly under the title Son of God.

Son of God

Background

Of itself 'Son of God' is a very vague title, capable of diverse uses. In the Old Testament there are primitive polytheistic and mythical uses (for example, Gen 6:2 and Deut 32:8). It is used of Israel chosen by God for his special purpose (for example, Hos 1:10) and so quoted by Paul (Rom 9:26); it is used also for an individual chosen for a special mission (the king in Ps 2:7, the judge in Ps 82:6). It never became a messianic title in Judaism, but was widely used in the Hellenistic world for mythical beings and for men of prominence.

Usage in the New Testament

The title is not in the kerygmatic speeches in Acts, but is otherwise widespread, and it becomes a matter of trying to clarify its content, or variety of contents, in the same author. Mark appears to give it a special sense. Mk 1:1 is textually doubtful, but would appear to make an inclusion with the declaration of the centurion: 'Truly this man was a son of God' (Mk 15:39), where one could distinguish Mark's meaning from the centurion's if the saying is authentic. It is used by devils (Mk 3:11), apparently trying to break the messianic secret. On the lips of the high priest (Mk 14:61) it is equivalent to 'Messiah'. The sense Mark intends to give it is that of the Messiah who triumphs through suffering and death – that is, Son of Man.

Matthew adds it to sayings where it is not in Mark or Luke: for him it has become a messianic title. It is often associated in the synoptics with the working of miracles, and so has taken on some of the colouring of the heavenly man. Paul uses it very widely and in a whole spectrum of senses from the most vague to the most suggestive of pre-existent Son (Gal 1:16 and 4:4; Rom 8:3). In John it is a divine figure throughout. Son of God is frequent and draws its content from the relation to the Father that is carefully spelled out (especially in Jn 8 and 10, leading up to the climaxes of Jn 10:30 and 10:38). Jesus defines his own 'sonship' repeatedly in terms of dependence on and obedience to the Father. In the farewell discourses he promises indwelling of Father, Son and Spirit. Peculiar to John is the direct attribution of 'God' to Christ: 'the Logos was God'. In Jn 1:18, the reading may be 'only [Son] God', or 'only Son'. It was necessary for *theos* to become somehow differentiated before this could happen. To the Jews *theos* is the Father in heaven and it is unthinkable that Jesus could have thought of himself as the Father.

'My lord and my God' (Jn 20:28) of Thomas is followed by the statement of the gospel's purpose, ' . . . the Christ the Son of God', so one might be right to see Thomas's confession as an equivalent to 'God the Son'.

It is clear that in the earliest kerygma Jesus became Son of God either in his resurrection or at his baptism, and in Romans he was 'constituted Son of God in power by the Holy Spirit' (Rom 1:1–4) at his resurrection (*cf* Acts 10:42). As we have seen, the title is particularly associated with miracles, release and manifestation of divine power. So he was seen to have become Son of God by the gift of the Spirit, to manifest God's power in his teaching and his miracles, and/or to release raising-from-the-dead power in his exaltation at God's right hand. So the title is first descriptive of *what* God does *through* him and only later of *who he is*. But the real or natural sonship does not displace the functional as something merely outgrown.

Kyrios, Lord

There has been much discussion of the background from which Christians drew the title 'Lord' for Christ. This only matters if the background somehow limits or defines its meaning. Four explanations of its origin are prominent:

(i) A Semitic secular milieu, the Aramaic *mar* like the Greek *Kyrios* simply means 'Sir', and Jesus is so addressed by many in the gospels. The evangelist may wish to suggest theological overtones, but this cannot be the only background as a title for Christ.

(ii) The Jewish Palestinian religious origin, the word being derived from *adon* (Hebrew) or *mare* used absolutely (the lord) for Yahweh by Palestinian Jews. But did they ever address or so speak to God? Bultmann[3] thought this absolute usage ('the lord' as opposed to 'my lord') unthinkable for a Jew. However, the Qumran manuscripts show evidence for *mare* (the lord) in some Old Testament texts.

(iii) The Hellenistic Jewish religious background where *ho Kyrios* was derived from the LXX usage, in which 'Kyrios' was translated 'Yahweh'. In fact the LXX texts of the time transliterated either as YHWH or IAΩ or ΠιΠi (PIPI), but they must have *said* when reading aloud, *ho Kyrios*, and most Jews only heard the Old Testament.

(iv) The pagan Hellenistic usage, common in cults for various divinities, which became increasingly a title for the emperor. Domitian (81–96 AD) was *dominus et deus* but the usage was earlier in the Eastern empire (Thomas's *Kyrios kai theos* could have come off a statue of Caius).

Bultmann thought Paul drew the title from this Hellenistic usage.[4] Certainly Paul knew of it (1 Cor 8:5–6), but he did not originate the title (*cf* Phil 2:11 and Acts 2:36). His use of it is to assert that Christ is Lord over all such 'lords', so the Hellenistic usage may have influenced Christian use.

It is unlikely that there was a single origin or uniform usage from the beginning. The chief argument for an Aramaic origin is the *maranatha* of 1 Cor 16:22, where *maran* equals 'Our lord', and so is not absolute (*cf* Rev 22:20). The fact that Paul, writing in Greek to Corinth, uses this liturgical expression shows that the Aramaic is the original.[5] In Paul it is the most pervasive of all titles. As 'Christ' became empty of theological content and became merely a surname (presumably because the Messiah idea would mean little or nothing to gentile converts), *Kyrios* took over the *content* of Christ. It is certainly always a title of the risen and exalted Christ (*cf* 1 Cor 11:26), where we do not celebrate the death of Jesus, but the risen Lord, so that the death and resurrection are held together. Phil 2:11 suggests that 'Jesus Christ is Lord' is the primitive creed, and this is corroborated by 1 Cor 12:3 and Rom 10:9, which are only intelligible if one realizes that Jesus became accursed by hanging on a tree (Deut 21:23), but of course did not remain accursed. It was the pervasive title because a summary of all that the risen Christ is and is expected to be, so not wholly distinct in meaning from other titles. Its special sense would appear to be that of mastery over all the powers that hold the world in thrall. So already in Phil 2:11. The Old Testament text that is repeatedly quoted in connection with Jesus becoming Lord in his exaltation is Ps 110:1 (*cf* Acts 2:34–6). In 1 Cor 15:23–8 the idea is worked out in full. Jesus preached the kingdom of God: he is not hailed as king in the New Testament, though there is passing reference to his reigning in 1 Cor 15:25; he subjects all powers beneath him – 'I make your enemies the footstool under your feet' – but he finally subjects himself to God. Among the most striking quotations from the Old Testament are those in which a passage referring to God as Kyrios is applied to Christ; for example, Acts 2:21 and Rom 10:13. But it would be a mistake to press too hard the implications of these texts, or the absolute use of *ho Kyrios* of Jesus. It remains a symbol of the function of the risen One to gather all into subjection to the Father.

Spirit

In the Old Testament the breath (*ruach*) of God is the creative source of all life (*cf* the Spirit in creation revivifying dead bones, Ez 37). Men survive by the communication of the Spirit (Ps 18:8–15; Hos 13:13–15; Is 30:27–8), moving us to saving deeds (Judg 3:10 and 1 Sam 11:6–13), causing havoc (Judg 9:23 and 1 Kings 22:23), anointing kings (1 Sam 10:10 and 16:13). The idea that the Spirit is the principle of prophetic utterance (inspiration) is largely a late usage, after the classical prophets (Ez 2:2, Zech 7:12). In earlier writings the Spirit causes the ecstatic state rather than the utterance, which is brought about by the word of God. There is expectation of the outpouring of the Spirit on the whole people (Is 32:15, 44:3–4; Ez 39:29; Joel 2:28–32).

In the New Testament in Luke and in Acts the Spirit is above all one of prophecy, an event rather than a possession or indwelling. Jesus is filled with the Spirit at his baptism (Lk 4:1) and announces his message in the power of the Spirit (Lk 4:14–39). At his exaltation he pours out his Spirit as his gift to the Church (Acts 2:4 and 2:33). The spread of the gospel is the work of the Spirit (Acts 1:8).

For Paul, the Spirit is indwelling (1 Cor 3:16, 6:15–17, and 12:27). The Spirit is *the* gift from which all other gifts flow (1 Cor 12:4–11 and Rom 5:5). He has two series of texts: those identifying the risen Christ with the activity of the Spirit (for example, 2 Cor 3:17, 'The lord is the Spirit . . . '; and note the equivalents in Rom 8:9–11); and triadic texts (for example, 2 Cor 13:13). 1 Cor 12:4–6 is triadic but 1 Cor 12:12–13 shows that the Spirit is the gift of the Kyrios.

The Trinitarian formula for baptism is given in Mt 28:19 and is also attested in the Didache, whereas earlier formulas are 'into the name of Jesus'. In John there is the Paraclete (Jn 14:15–17, 14:25–6, and 15:26–7; see also Jn 16:7–14, which are two versions of the same address). He is identified as the Holy Spirit in Jn 14:26. Another Paraclete (Jesus himself is the first) is mentioned in 1 Jn 2:1, Rom 8:34, and Heb 7:25. The word has various meanings and John uses them all: as interpreter or teacher the Paraclete leads into all truth and guides them to see the true meaning of Jesus rather than revealing new truths; as witness to Jesus he guides their understanding of him, so that they witness to him in their preaching and in the signs they will perform.

As advocate with the Father he sees that their prayers for their missions are granted, a role Jesus says he will perform himself; and he is consoler of the disciples in the Lord's absence.

The Spirit is also the spring of life within those who believe (*cf* Jn 4:10 and 7:37–9); Jn 7:39 makes explicit that in both passages Jesus is speaking of the Spirit, the source of eternal life. This is very like the Pauline doctrine of the indwelling Spirit, and should be connected with the promise of Jesus to abide in the believer (Jn 17) and with the consoler.

So, for both John and Paul, the Spirit is the way Jesus chooses to dwell in and give life to the believer (Jn 7:39).

The first act of the risen Lord is to give his Spirit (Jn 20:22) and some would see 'he handed over the Spirit' (Jn 19:30) as meaning the same, and 'He breathed on them' as God in creation (Gen 2:7), making a new creation, new life. They are made the community of reconciliation, a reference to the whole mission of the Son, rather than to particular acts of forgiveness, such as baptism.

In the Pauline churches the gifts of the Spirit were very much a matter of *experience*, not just a theorem, a doctrine to be assented to. To what extent do John's passages also assume that the Christian experiences the Spirit? The roles of witness, teacher, consoler, all suggest this, as does Jn 7:39 ('There was as yet no Spirit because Jesus was not yet risen from the dead') – that is, the spring had not yet come.

Baptism, Eucharist, Penance

Baptism and Confirmation

Baptism was customary in the first century BC as a rite by which proselytes were received into the synagogue, signifying the cleansing of the impure, and showed forth forgiveness of sin because people were transferred to God's people.

John the Baptist startles by preaching baptism for Jews and demanding repentance from them. His baptism was preceded by confession of sin (Mk 1:4–5) and a resolution of conversion (cf his message to the different classes of men who questioned him). In Mt 3:2, 'Repent for the kingdom of God is at hand', is a summary of John the Baptist's teaching, and readiness to be baptized by him would be an outward sign of acknowledgement of sinfulness, a conversion of heart and expectation of God's coming kingdom.

All four evangelists set John at the beginning of the gospel and see him as fundamental to the inauguration of Christian life, not that his baptism is Christian baptism, but Christ himself enters into the process inaugurated by John and brings it to its full reality and meaning.

Matthew adds two verses (Mt 3:14–15) to Mark's account to explain the difficulty seen in Jesus submitting to a rite that was a confession of sinfulness, but the explanation was obscure. What emerges from the whole story is that, at the outset of his ministry, Jesus is identified with sinners. He is identified by the voice from heaven, and the dove descending on him, as the servant of Is 42:1, and the identification is carried further (Jn 1:29) where John the Baptist declares

Jesus to be 'the lamb of God who takes away the sin of the world' (cf Is 53:7–12, where the servant is proclaimed as suffering and is compared to a sacrificial lamb and said to bear the iniquity of all). Incidentally, in Matthew and Mark only Jesus sees the vision and hears the voice, but in Luke and John, John the Baptist sees and hears and testifies.

Christian Baptism

John proclaims one who will immerse in the Spirit (Mk 1:8), not only in water but in the Spirit and in fire (Jn 1:33; Mt 3:11; Lk 3:16), which may be an allusion to the coming of the Spirit at Pentecost in the form of tongues of fire, or may be a general reference to the Day of Judgement, signifying the finality of Jesus' baptism.

Important differences, then, are that it imparts the Spirit (Jn 1:33) and that it takes away sin (Jn 1:29). In Acts 1:5, Jesus himself after the resurrection is reported as telling the apostles that Pentecost will be their baptism in the Holy Spirit.

Institution of Baptism by Christ

John equivalently proclaimed, 'I have baptized you in water, but he will baptize you in the Holy Spirit' (Mk 1:8). There is an express command of Jesus (Mt 28:19), though some think this is a late addition.

In Jn 4:1 Jesus had already had people baptized by the disciples, while John the Baptist continued to baptize. But is this Christian baptism in the full sense or a sign of Jesus joining his disciples?

Baptism and the Imposition of Hands

The Apostolic Church signified the gift of the Spirit, not only by baptism but by the imposition of hands; and various incidents show some tendency of the two rites to come apart and for baptism to be understood as forgiving sins but imposition of hands for giving the Spirit. On the day of

Pentecost, Peter's words echo the preaching of John, and put together baptism, forgiveness, and the gift of the Spirit.

But Acts 8:12 show Philip (the deacon) baptizing and the apostles coming to give the Spirit later, which suggests that only the apostles could give the Spirit. However, Acts 10:44 shows the Spirit given first without imposition of hands and baptism follows, while Acts 19:1 has the baptism of John the Baptist persisting.

In Jn 3:3–5 there is emphasis that the two cannot be separated. What held the three together was the emerging Christian understanding that baptism does not *now* signify merely cleansing from sin, but immersion in the death and resurrection of Christ – that is, that sins are forgiven by the gift of his Spirit.

Christian Understanding of Baptism

Our Lord foretold his coming death as a baptism (Mk 10:38; Lk 12:50), the classic text being Rom 6:3–11, and a similar understanding underlies Gal 5:24–5, though baptism is not specifically mentioned. John's gospel was written as news of new creation (*cf* Jn 1:19 to 2:11, with the days of the new creation indicated). The theme is made explicit in the meeting with Nicodemus, with its ambiguity between 'anew' and 'from above'. The whole of 1 Pet 1:3–14 is a baptismal exhortation (*cf* 1 Pet 1:23 and 2:2). In Gal 6:15, there is 'new creation', not with any express reference to baptism, but in contrast to circumcision (*cf* 2 Cor 5:17; Jas 1:18).

Incorporation into Christ is a further expression, and in 1 Cor 12:13 there is 'drink of one Spirit', recalling the 'fountains of living water' (Jn 4:14 and Eph 4:4). 1 Cor sees the prototype of this in the crossing of the Red Sea: by baptism a New People is formed – not just an operation on an individual. For baptism into Christ (not Trinitarian) see Gal 3:27 and Rom 13:14, where the white garment is mentioned.

Other ideas are: illumination (Eph 5:14) which recalls the baptismal candle; cleansing and purifying, in a burial context (Eph 5:25–7), and sprinkling of blood on the Day of

Atonement (Heb 10:22); the seal of the Spirit, the seal of membership of God's people (the word used being a tally on a sack which is a first instalment, to assure that the rest is to follow).

Baptism and Confirmation

It will be seen that there is a great richness of thought in the New Testament about the meaning of Christian initiation, but it remains one reality. There does not seem to be a basis for thinking of two distinct acts of initiation conferring two separate effects. In the East the two sacraments are given together, confirmation being seen as the sign of growth with baptism as that of birth.

A great deal of argument has arisen about infant baptism: Catholics argue that whole households were baptized which must have included children; and Baptists say that it is not attested in scripture. In fact, 1 Cor 7:14 makes clear that, in Paul's thorough 'body theology', a child was in the body by being born from one Christian parent and, as there is no mention of baptism one assumes that the child was not thought to be in need of it.

Eucharist

The synoptics make clear that Jesus ate the Paschal supper on the Thursday evening, but John shows that on the Friday the Pharisees had not yet eaten it (Jn 18:28). John moves the day so that Jesus would die when the Paschal lambs were being sacrificed in the temple. Luke has Jesus' farewell discourse (Lk 22:14–18) comparable to that of John (Jn 13–17); the two strophes end with the idea of fulfilment in the kingdom of God. This eschatological reference is echoed in 1 Cor 11:26. Some see here a vow of Jesus and understand it as a self-dedication to the Passover of his resurrection.

In the institution narratives, which fall into two groups (Matthew-Mark and Paul), each reflecting the liturgy used in different churches, the Jewish meal blessing is used – both 'blessed' and 'gave thanks' – with the Passover blessing of the cup including an intercession for God's people.

Paul uses 'body', like any Jew, to indicate not a separate component but 'a whole of experience', as we experience ourselves as a body, both as flesh-body (liable to physical and moral weakness) and as a spirit-body. A 'spirit-body' (a contradiction in terms to a Greek) means 'open to the action of God', so the idea of distinguishing the body from the blood (body contains blood) is misplaced.

Jeremiah promised the 'new covenant' (Jer 31:31) and Jesus' words evoke Exodus where Moses sprinkles the blood on the altar and on the people (Ex 24:6); 'for the remission of sins' (Matthew only) connects Paschal supper and Passion with the Day of Atonement. 'Do this as my memorial', about which Max Thurian wrote to show that the Jews thought they made the past present and stood with their forefathers in the exodus.[1] 'Proclaim the death of the Lord until he comes' does not refer to the mortal Jesus, as Paul is holding together the mortal Jesus and his risen state.

There are no arguments for realism from 'this is my body' for Aramaic has no copula. That the Eucharist was understood as a sacrificial meal can be seen in Corinthians: here (1 Cor 10:17–22) 'altar' means God, his portion being laid on the altar while the offerer took his own home, and a sacrifice being a sharing of a meal with God.

So John, in the discourse on the bread of life (Jn 6); it is odd that the Pharisees present should have asked for a sign, when Jesus had worked the feeding of the 5,000 only the night before. But they want a sign from heaven, to show that the authority of Jesus supersedes that of Moses. Jesus replies that the sign they are looking for is himself: 'I am the bread of life.'

Hebrews probably has no reference to the Eucharist, but is important for Eucharistic doctrine because of its conception of Christ's priesthood (Heb 9:14 and 9:23–6). On the Day of Atonement, the high priest enters through the veil into the holy of holies to rub blood on the covering of the

ark, with the idea that Christ entered once for all the heavenly sanctuary to pour his blood there (the writer, probably
Apollos, is using platonic ideas for the 'true heaven' and
the 'this-worldly'); the 'once for all' is not simply in the
past but is entry into eternity. Jesus exercises his priesthood
through the Eucharist, gathering us into the movement of
his self-offering.[2]

Penance and the Anointing of the Sick

The preoccupation of the New Testament is with the call to
faith in Christ and to baptism for forgiveness of sin. Early
expectation of the Parousia did not raise questions of the
forgiveness of post-baptismal sin. Did the post-apostolic
Church believe that such sin could be forgiven at all? Jn
20:21–3 is taken as the equivalent of Mt 18:18, and translated into terms that non-Jews would understand, nor is it
clear that it has reference beyond baptism and conversion
to Christianity and application to the post-baptismal sins of
Christians. Nonetheless, the saying placed here is a striking
commission to the apostles.

In Mt 16:19, there is the special position given to Peter as
a response to his profession of faith: the keys are the symbol of authority over the household so that the holder can
let in or shut out. Neither this saying nor Mt 18:18 specify
anything about sin, to bind and loose being used of strict or
more pliant interpretation of the law (Shammai binds and
Hillel looses).

However, Mt 18:18 is about the treatment of Christian
offenders, and there is reason to think that Jn 20:21 gives
the meaning of the phrase, so that it means the power to
excommunicate in a way that will be ratified by God. This
interpretation is supported by Jewish practice for the
Sanhedrin had power to admit or readmit (*cf* the man born
blind).

It is also corroborated by Paul's action at Corinth.

To sum up: there is no New Testament evidence for the
forgiveness of post-baptismal sins; the apostolic age was

certainly faced with the question of the notorious sinner and there is more evidence for exclusion than for readmission. We can see in extreme cases the basis of the idea that flagrant sin involves a break with the Christian community, and that forgiveness is reconciliation with the Church, not just a matter of private relationship to God.

Anointing of the Sick

In Mark, the anointing of the sick (Mk 6:13) is a common custom amongst both Jews and pagans, especially in the case of the possessed, and comes here after 'cast out devils', so the disciples of Jesus used the practice as a sign of the messianic times.

In James, the sick man is to be anointed with oil (Jas 5:14–16), such as the Good Samaritan poured on the man's wounds. The role of the elders should be noted since James does not recommend a charismatic healing. Healing of the sick was prominent in Jesus' ministry and in the mission he gave to the disciples (*cf* Mk 16:17–18).

Baptism in the Patristic Age

There is only desultory evidence until the third century, but baptism is seen as sealing the person as a Christian and as sealing the covenant of his or her admission to the Christian people. The tendency, however, appears to think of baptism as a washing rather than a plunging into the death of Christ. This makes it possible to think of the washing as forgiving sin, and the subsequent ritual as giving the Spirit.

This possibility lay more in some rites than in others. Hippolytus has the following order: baptism; priest's anointing or signing in the name of Christ; bishop's imposition of hands; bishop's anointing.[3]

This order of precedence is not attested to outside Rome at this time, but came in later in the East only to drop out again. Hence, for the East, baptism equals confirmation.

Separate action by the bishop tended to dissociate the giving of the Spirit from forgiveness of sins. Tertullian, using the African model, says the priest's anointing gives the seal and the bishop's laying on of hands the Spirit.[4]

Throughout the re-baptism controversy of the third century all assert that only the true Church can give the Spirit. The idea is foreshadowed in the anonymous third century *De Rebaptismate* that, while the priest's anointing gives the Spirit in the basic sense, later rites by the bishop give a more perfect gift of the Spirit.

Augustine develops this idea in soldierly metaphors, which lead to the conviction that the bishop's imposition of hands is adult initiation, which was not so in the East. One must see sacraments as an unfolding by the Church of what she is and what is essential to her life.

The Church lives the sacraments before theorizing or classifying them.

As to institution by Christ, the idea is covered by the developing understanding by the Church, guided by the Spirit, of what Christ intended for his Church in founding her.

Character

The idea of character originated from Augustine's 'seal', and is mainly associated with the priest's anointing or signing in the name of Christ – though Cyril of Jerusalem speaks of the 'water giving the seal'.[5] The elements of the idea of character will, then, include unrepeatability and that man is marked as Christ's (Augustine's seal refers to the brand mark on an emperor's soldier), that this has eschatological reference (*cf* Eph 4:30; see also Rev 7:2 and 9:4) and can count for or against one on the Day of Judgment.

No one person in the third century ever suggested there were two marks for the acts of anointing or imposition. If a certain writer speaks of the character given by anointing, it is not clear whether he is thinking of the water or the signing rites: the latter in the West is part of anointing, but equals imposition of hands in the East. It is not necessary to think of any internal entity being imprinted; any past event of my history is indelible, such as a vow of religion or marriage.

Rebaptism and Validity

Controversy arose in the third century with Novatian, and in the fourth century with Donatus, over the question of schism. Did a schismatic Church baptize effectively or did a convert from schism have to be re-baptized, no one thinking a person could be baptized twice?

The African tradition advocated by Cyprian until the time of Augustine clung to the idea that, as only the true Church could give the Spirit, schismatics had cut themselves off and so did not effectively baptize. This was the thesis of Donatists who at the same time said *they* were the true Church. Meanwhile, Rome and the general tradition of the Church held that, as the Names had been spoken over the person, even in schismatic or heretical baptism, this could not be repeated.

Augustine upholds the Roman tradition, saying that anointing could not be repeated, as something definitive had been done, and so it was *valid*, but it was ineffective as it did not give the Spirit or forgive sins. A converted heretic needs the laying on of hands for this.

The Eucharist in the Patristic Age

Realist language and the idea of sacrifice are found in the Didache, and Justin speaks of 'the food which has been made the Eucharist'[6] being the flesh and blood of Christ.

Among symbolic language the *Apostolic Constitutions* speak of the mysteries as antitypes of the body and blood, showing the Eastern tendency to identify symbol and symbolized. Both languages are sometimes used by the same author, as in the case of Augustine's sermon 227, with an insistence on spiritual reception ('to receive is to believe') and finally he quasi-identifies the Eucharistic body with the Church which could suggest that the shared meal is simply a symbol of our existing unity in Christ. Consecration is described variously as by the use of Jesus' words or by invocation of the Spirit, as the Orthodox Church understands; but there are two kinds of *epiclesis*, the consecratory and that for the fruits of the Eucharist, and in some liturgies the consecratory comes before the institution narrative, as the whole Eucharistic prayer is regarded as consecratory without there being any 'moment' of consecration.

Conversion or change language originates in the Eastern Fathers and from them passes to Ambrose. There is a whole string of 'trans-' words, so transubstantiation is only one of a long list. We have seen that sacrificial language is used very early, it is spiritual by comparison with the material sacrifices of Jews and pagans, a fulfilment of Malachi. But the elements are offered, not just words and praises. Early liturgies reflect this theology.

As late as the ninth century, a great protest came from Paschasius Radbertus at the attempt to separate what the Church had always held together, the Eucharistic and historical body of Christ. Later patristic thought was too occupied with proving the real presence and sacrifice.

The Development of Penance

The discipline of penance consisted in confession of sins to a bishop who declared excommunication and admission to the ranks of penitent, a place at the back of the church in penitential garments, and exclusion from presence at the Eucharist (in the East, though only from reception in the West).

After the prescribed period the bishop reconciled by the laying on of hands. There were varying lists of sins, the Synod of Elvira prescribing up to ten years.

Lent originates as a general penitential time for the whole Church, fused with the final preparations of catechumens for Easter. Monastic therapeutic confession arose in the East and was transplanted to the West by Cassian and was not regarded as a sacrament.

Summary

There was a struggle in the heroic age between the idea of God's mercy and that of the communion of saints. To offend God scandalously is to hurt the body of Christ, so forgiveness is reconciliation with the Church. The sacraments were seen as basic principles in the life of the Church, and not as God-to-man actions bypassing the Church, and as conferring status in and relation to the people. Hence the inseparable connection between baptism, penance, Eucharist. Reconciled heretics were not given baptism, because their baptism had now 'taken'.

For much of what later came to be called mortal sins there was no action by the Church, no exclusion from the Eucharist, which itself forgives sins (as Trent said), but only exhortations to repentance, fasting and the like. The severe discipline defeated its own object, and resulted in the postponement of baptism and of penance until one's deathbed, so that perplexities arose if a person recovered. Penance ceases to be part of the Church's life and becomes a preparation for death. Scholastic theology came to think of penance as a judicial process, the judgment being of what penance to give and of fitness for reconciliation. Private confession was brought in by the monks in the seventh century, the heir to monastic therapeutic confession, the sacrament being used for spiritual guidance and renewal.

The question arose, does the Church forgive sins? Patristic thought is very elusive about whether reconciliation *conveys* God's forgiveness or *assures* that he forgives. The main reason for the doubt is that to forgive sin included having done the penance. There were strands of rigorism, denying that the Church could ever restore the peace of the Church for certain sins, but not denying that God forgives them. But this was true of those who had already confessed to the bishop or priest and had asked for penance. If a person had not done this they would not be thought to have any private access to God's forgiveness.

Development of Sacramental Theology

In the eleventh century, Berengarius of Tours held that a sign cannot *be* what it signifies, so the bread and wine are not the body of Christ but represent them (logical positivism started by Abelard!). Berengarius is chiefly interesting for exposing the crudely materialistic ideas of the time and for giving impetus to the development of sacramental theology.

A threefold division developed between the *sacramentum tantum, res et sacramentum* and *res tantum,* as in the case of the Eucharistic elements. The origin of the idea is that a sacrament can be duly conferred without giving grace and so be unrepeatable. The 'character' in baptism is an example. Because unrepeatable the character was extended to confirmation, order and marriage, and also covers the notion of reviviscence. Hence the idea of *res et sacramentum* covers four things:

—The sacraments are God's sovereign actions in the Church and it is the faith of the Church which effects them, not that of the minister or recipient.
— They are objectively conferred even if the dispositions of the receiver prevent them having the effect of conferring grace.
—This explains the unrepeatability of 'character' sacraments . . .
—and it also explains reviviscence.

This idea is the basis of the doctrine of validity, for if the sacrament 'works' it is conferred and has its effect on the receiver. But there are objections: the historical event being sufficient, what is meant by an invisible entity (a sort of transfer that children play with)? The *res et sacramentum* is a misnomer, as an invisible reality cannot be a sign (in a marriage a peculiar reality hovering between bride and groom).

The terminology *ex opere operato* (or *operantis*) stressed the objective nature of what was done, like a pouring jug; you receive according to the size of the pot put under the drinks machine, but God's action is not limited to that of the Church, rather is it guaranteed by it. Man's readiness to receive the gift is necessary if he is to receive it, but not the cause of the gift itself, for Christ is made truly present by a bad priest.

The intention of the minister was generally accepted: he must intend to do what the Church does and intends, because more is required than an intention to go through the Church's motions. The two poles of the discussion, then, are a pagan baptizing at the request of a Christian and the Christian minister acting, but having a contrary intention, though it may be doubted whether the latter makes any difference: theologians wriggle, saying God or the Church supplies, but it comes to the same thing. What is required is that the action should be sufficiently human to be the Church's.

Can the interior, unmanifested and contrary intention of a perverse minister prevent it being the Church's action? Most theologians think it can, but there remains a doubt on the point, and part of the difficulty arises from trying to find a lowest common multiple for all sacraments; whereas true internal consent is necessary for marriage it does not follow that it is so for all sacraments. For example, the definition of Trent of intending to do what the Church does, does not define the content of the intention very exactly. It is aimed at, and excludes, Luther's assertion that it is the faith of the recipient which determines what is received, regardless of what the minister does or does not do. Very little is said about the faith of the recipient.

Theologians seem undecided whether infant baptism is a case apart or provides a rule applicable in all cases. The minimum view is that the sacrament is conferred where it does not find the obstacle of a contrary will. A lot of the discussion seems to be about fringe cases, but sacraments should be understood in terms of the normal. Are all sacraments what they are in the same way? Has not theology made a mistake in trying to define the lowest common multiple? The common factor is the Church as an effective sign of God's saving action.

Even granted that all conditions are fulfilled, the sacrament does not produce its effect because this is so, but because God is faithful to his promises: his action is not confined or limited to the usual channels, for these are the assurance of his action, but absence of these conditions is not an assurance of absence of his action.

Questions of the form 'Did anything happen?', 'Is he a priest?', 'Were they married?', are not directly answerable. Theologians seem to have struggled for the kind of certainty that is not to be had, but could only come from testing the actual effect. It follows that one cannot conclude from the Church's witholding assurance that no effect can have taken place.

Transsubstantiation

The word 'transubstantiation' is one of a long line of such words, conveying an objective change or conversion of the elements; it can be traced back to the eleventh century and so is not wedded to Aristotelianism. Nothing is added by the word to the Church's faith, but Aristotelian philosophy is no longer understood; the real accidents remain, not the appearance of them, so not all the bread is changed but only the substance. It expresses a mystery and no words are adequate.

Luther's protest is against the extrinsicism of Catholic sacramental life and reliance on ritual in place of faith. But, as the Catholic Church taught clearly that sacraments do not produce grace without the proper dispositions of the recipient, it is not always easy to see the force of Luther's complaint.

The general direction of reformed theology is to assert that faith causes the reception of grace, and to deny that sacraments are different from preaching (Luther understood sacrament as the mere sign after his nominalist instruction by such as Gabriel Biel), both being means to arouse faith. This is clearer in Calvin than in Luther.

A Good Conscience

Conscience

By 'conscience' is meant our power of moral judgment, of discerning good from bad in human behaviour, of deciding right and wrong courses of action, particularly in complex situations where different and conflicting values are at stake.

'Moral values' should not be understood in a narrow sense, least of all as restricted to sexual matters. Nor are moral values simply private ones as opposed to public issues. All human values are in some sense moral, though the moral component in different areas may be greater or less. For instance, it is part of the duty of the State to promote, though not necessarily to control, education and the arts: these are human and therefore moral values and needs. It may well be thought that the moral component is greater in education than in the arts, but some moral values are involved in both areas. And it will certainly be argued as a human and moral issue to what extent the State should exercise control over education: it should certainly ensure that children receive as good an education as possible, for their sake and for the sake of society's future. But should not the content of education be controlled by the educators, university and other teachers, and not (for instance) by a political party in power which is perhaps concerned mainly about the country's material and industrial prosperity?

From these considerations will easily be seen the falsity of the slogan that the Church should keep to the sacristy (to worship) and out of politics. The Church should certainly not align itself with any particular political party or programme; its task is to challenge all programmes by the gospel and to approve what makes for the establishment of Christ's lordship in human life, but also to criticize the best that human intelligence can devise insofar as it still falls short of the Kingdom. The Church is therefore bound to have an interest in education and has always played a leading part in its development at every level; the Church has, too, always taken a prominent role in promoting music and other arts, as it has in health care. And, of course, in all that concerns the family it must be deeply involved. Indeed, everything affecting society is political and the Church is necessarily involved.

Conscience must not be thought of as some sort of insulated 'black box' lodged somewhere inside us, which records what is right or wrong for us without reference to external facts and considerations. It is not some kind of hot-line to God or intervention of his Spirit, but an operation of our reason which must deal with facts and reasons. The privacy and ultimacy of the individual conscience do not imply any such insulation or guarantee, but rather our ability and responsibility to make our own decisions.

The main authority in any situation demanding moral judgment and decision is that of the facts – not merely all that we can discover about any given situation, but all we can foretell about the expected consequences of different courses of action. Facts have to be worked for and argued about, though we will never be able to discover all that is relevant or be certain of probable outcomes, and will have to work with approximations and probabilities. There can be no justification in the appeal to 'my rights of conscience', if I have not taken the trouble to discover all I can about present facts and future probabilities. For instance, a psychiatrist may be faced with the question of abortion in the case of a deeply disturbed patient who is pregnant: he may be morally certain that, if she has a baby, she will kill herself, or the baby, or both. There are surely cases where only the expert has any ability to assess the facts.

The dictum that one cannot logically pass from a statement of fact to one of obligation has continually been repeated: an 'is' cannot give rise to an 'ought'. The dictum is simply false. Whatever may be the case in other areas, the field of morals has its own logic, as may be seen from the simple example: 'She is my mother, so I ought to go and see her.'

Authority lies not only in facts but in reasons. Moral judgment is not insulated from all our other areas of awareness and judgment, but interacts with them in a process of mutual conditioning. Indeed, our moral evaluations are first social and corporate before they are individual and personal. We first absorb the moral standards and conventions of the family and society into which we are born; these provide the material out of which our evaluations can be formed, and we can only progressively come either to make them personally our own or to wish to modify or overthrow them. I could be born into a class which regards the poor as improvident, irresponsible or criminally inclined, and only by degrees, with growing knowledge of social conditions, come to espouse their cause as deprived and unjustly oppressed. One may note in passing that our moral philosophy has been over-individualistic, concentrating on the obligations (for example, from promises) of individuals and taking too little account of social forces and communal responsibilities. It has been for theology to become aware of corporate or structural sin, something of which the Old Testament was keenly aware before it ever came to a recognition of individual responsibility.

If enough people challenge the moral values of society, they will in time change the generally accepted values – for better or for worse. In my own lifetime, it can be argued, some values have been changed for the worse. The law exists to reflect and support the values society actually holds in any ways in which society wishes them to be supported, not to dictate its values to society. But the law is regarded as having a certain majesty, as commanding respect and awe. Hence to change the law can result in a change in society's evaluation. This can clearly be seen in the cases of divorce and abortion. If a course of action is legal, not against the law, it is not therefore morally right:

adultery is a case in point. But if divorce becomes legally possible, then by swift transitions it comes to be regarded as socially acceptable and then morally right, with the result that more and more marriages end in divorce. As has been said, it is not the function of the lawgiver to tell society what its values should be, but law inevitably tends to have this effect. Hence the lawgiver should be aware of this factor and take a very conservative attitude to relaxations of laws which may be in some respects too rigid.

Conscience Does Not Work Deductively

The classical natural law theory, which has predominated in Catholic moral theology, sought to establish *universal premisses* from which we could read off our obligations in particular instances, and hence saw moral judgment as operating deductively. This type of moral theology came in with scholasticism; that is, an age when the dominating ideas were law and the syllogism.

The universal premisses, however, cannot be established. This could only be done: either if every conceivable instance were considered and its moral qualities discerned – which is obviously impossible of achievement; or if the universal premiss was itself deduced from another and self-evident universal – which was the method attempted. An example is that of truth telling: it was argued that to say what you know to be untrue is a case of frustrating a (God-given) faculty; but it is always wrong to frustrate the purpose(s) God has implanted in a faculty – so it is always wrong to say what you know to be untrue. We may pass over the fact that the major premiss is loaded by use of the idea of frustration: God could give more than one purpose, and to use a faculty for other than its more obvious purpose is not necessarily to frustrate it, only to enlarge its uses. It is the minor premiss that is at fault: it begs the question at issue, namely whether it is *always* wrong to frustrate a faculty, a question that can only be decided by inspection of particular cases, especially those which give rise to some doubt. The premiss may prove to hold in the majority of cases, but that is not to say it has universal validity. This point will be clarified in the next section.

This *a priori* approach to truthfulness was never able to cater for examples like Father Christmas or All Fools' Day. If there are 'jocose' exceptions to the rule it is not a universal, and there may well be exceptions of other kinds.

In a very broad sense there is truth in the idea of natural law. Different types of conduct are good or bad, right or wrong, because of the sort of beings we are; but this does not enable one to solve particular cases of difficulty. Generosity and unselfishness are laudable, but it does not follow that you should give money to everyone who asks; we have to decide by trying to discern cases that are genuine and deserving, and by calculating what may be done with the money we give.

The chief flaw in the classical natural law theory is that it takes too narrow a view of nature by limiting itself to the physical function or biological level, and not taking account of rational, fully human and psychological factors. At the biological level it is true that speech exists (was created by God, if one takes a religious view) to enable human communication, and that this is frustrated or impeded or defeated by untruth. But there may well be human situations (telling patients they are going to die, social conventions) which at least give one pause. At the biological level one can say that sexual intercourse exists to perpetuate the human race. But there are clearly human and personal factors at work as well, and these are just as much part of 'nature'. And it is noteworthy that the encyclical *Humanae Vitae* on family planning quietly set aside the teaching of *Casti Conubii* that procreation is the 'primary end' of marriage, whereas mutual solace is only 'secondary' and must give way. Most acts of intercourse are incapable of producing a child, and the factors of mutual love and support and commitment predominate.

Nor is it correct to say that 'artificial' methods of birth regulation are 'against nature', thereby meaning they must be morally wrong. 'Nature' includes human reasoning and the skills that God's gift of reason has enabled mankind to acquire. Nature is not a process that works perfectly for the good of mankind, and the whole science of medicine is geared to changing the course of nature for the benefit of human beings.

Hence any method of birth control must be evaluated in all its aspects and in the cases of particular couples. As with all complex moral questions, there will be good and bad features; one has to weigh the preponderance of one over the other, amass and assess facts, and cannot descend from above with ready-made answers.

One might also argue that the natural law theory operates with a timeless and unhistorical view of human nature, characteristic of the philosophy of the schools which developed under Greek influence. But has not human nature changed and developed over the centuries, and indeed millenia, of human evolution? Do we today think of human nature as a constant reality shared equally by primitive tribal humanity and contemporary urban and industrial mankind? Teilhard de Chardin[1] ran into trouble with his vision of human consciousness emerging from a rudimentary state and progressing to its present state of heightened awareness combined with great material complexification – and indeed still moving towards a more global and social consciousness on its way to its Omega point in the Kingdom of Christ.

A great deal of confusion, and indeed distress, has been generated by misuse of the phrase 'intrinsically evil' as equivalent to 'always and in all circumstances unallowable and wrong'.

The original and correct use is in opposition to 'extrinsically evil'. If it is forbidden to eat meat on Friday, then it is extrinsically evil to do so (evil by extended designation), but it is not intrinsically evil (internally in itself). The word 'intrinsically' morally adds nothing: if a course of action has bad features, they are really bad, intrinsically bad; but it does not at all follow that the action must be wrong in all sets of circumstances. As has been said in the case of birth control, the particular features of each individual case have to be considered and evaluated as the only rational way to reach a decision, and one may have to put up with some (intrinsically) bad features for the sake of greater good.

Finally, under this consideration of deductive ethics, we must consider a class of propositions which are tautologous, uninformative and of no use in reaching decisions. Examples are 'lying is [always] wrong'; so with 'cruelty', 'murder', etc. The words already convey moral disapproval, so to say they are 'wrong' merely draws out what has been said already. They are no more helpful in solving cases than similar positive terms such as 'generosity', 'unselfishness', 'kindness', etc. To reach a decision about difficult cases, one has first to describe them in neutral or non-judgmental language, which may be a cumbersome process. Lying is always wrong by definition, but there are surely cases where it is not wrong to say what you know to be untrue: I have already adverted to jocose instances, but others come to mind, such as that of a spy in wartime. Adultery is always wrong by definition, but one could only assert that 'sexual intercourse between a man and a woman at least one of whom was married to someone else' was *always* wrong, if one had considered every conceivable situation. It may be hard to think of a doubtful one; but that of the commissar who says to the wife, 'If you don't sleep with me, I'll have your husband framed on a spy charge and sent to a concentration camp' at least gives one pause. To say that that would not be adultery, or what one normally means by adultery, is to admit that you do not in that case disapprove, namely that there can be cases where the action described non-judgmentally would be legitimate.

Conscience Works Inductively

One can see that conscience or moral judgment operates inductively by considering its actual development in the course of growth from childhood to maturity. A child comes to recognize a moral value or disvalue, and the imperative that goes with it, in particular instances. For example, a boy may pull the cat's tail or pull the wings off of flies until he comes to realize that this is wrong, is cruel.

The boy is not merely told so, but comes to see it for himself – comes to see that it is wrong to tell lies, for example, to avoid punishment, because parents and children will never be able to trust each other if they tell each other lies.

The recognition in a given instance gives rise to a general idea (cruelty, lying) which will have further applications. A child can then become very literal and embarrassing about truth-telling: for example, when Aunt Alice foolishly asks, 'Did you like the book I gave you?' And it may be difficult to convey that it is all right to say, 'Mummy is not at home', when she is not feeling well and is resting. Other cases will then come to the growing person's experience, and he or she will thereby learn that each has to be discerned and evaluated in terms of its particular circumstances and aspects.

So moral judgment matures and becomes more sensitive and more flexible by consideration of particular cases: that is, it does so inductively. Early experience establishes a general idea or *principle*, and later experience has to decide whether it can always be applied literally or may sometimes need to be deepened and modified. From first notions of cruelty or respect for the feelings of others consideration will have to be given to such matters as: fighting other children; boxing at amateur or professional level; defending oneself and others, or property; maintaining law and order; war; the struggle for justice and against oppression; inflicting suffering on animals to advance medical knowledge. Principles may well operate as (universal) rules for the majority of cases I encounter (I pay my bus fares), but may need to be modified when I meet with novel features.

Conflict of Values

The moral issues which come up for discussion are not those in which all the good is on one side and all the bad on the other, but those which are patchy and a mixture of conflicting values: there will be good and bad on both sides – or multiple sides, according to the available options. Can one rightly combat terrorism by imprisonment without trial, when it is impossible to get witnesses to come forward even when a suspect's guilt is morally certain? Or, apart from the danger of imprisoning an innocent person, does such a procedure endanger the whole fabric of justice to an extent that does more harm than acts of terrorism? And it is futile to argue such a case as a back-seat driver. One has to ask: 'What would I decide, if I were in the hot seat and had to take responsibility for the decision and for the outcome?' Equally futile are those arguments where one person emphasizes the good (or bad) only on one side, and another person simply does the same for the other side.

It is of crucial importance in this connection to sort out the distinction between 'good/bad' on the one hand and 'right/wrong' on the other. In complex cases good and bad features will exist in different proportions on both sides.

What is 'right' and therefore obligatory (what I should do) is the course of action where you consider the preponderance of good to lie. And there is no correct answer somewhere at the end of a book. Different people will judge differently according to their own background, experience, political options, etc. In a true sense, in making a decision you are making yourself, you are deciding who you are. For example, in limited contact with those actually dealing with drug abusers I have found them in favour of legalizing cannabis. Young people see it as hypocritical to make the use of cannabis illegal (their drug) while alcohol is freely available (respectable society's drug). Because cannabis is illegal they are drawn into the criminal scene and soon come up against pushers who will get them onto amphetamines and then to more dangerous drugs.

And in such situations of conflicting values, as always, it is of paramount importance to discover as much as possible about the facts; for example, in cases of drug abuse, abortion, atomic weapons, euthanasia – both the generally applicable facts and also those proper to the particular case. It is impossible to exhaust all the facts, so one will always have to decide on probabilities, less than complete evidence. Further uncertainty arises from the need to forecast probable consequences. This is an essential element in the so-called 'just war' theory which, however, has its own weaknesses.

Facts lead to reasons, and one tries to decide in terms of overriding reasons. One will argue that any reasonable person, surveying the facts and the arguments, will decide one way. This is what Kant meant by saying that the maxim for my actions should be universal, that is, applicable to any rational person as such.[2]

Objectivity

And that is what objectivity in moral judgment consists in – having public reasons based on carefully assessed facts. Proponents of deductive ethics seek rather for an external norm against which moral judgments may be measured, to ensure objectivity and the certainty of moral decision. For them the 'right reason' is moral judgment which grasps the unchanging rules of conduct which derive from our nature, and a good conscience is one that has been formed by these rules and has put them into practice. But it must be doubted whether any such certainty is to be had. Our human condition is limited and must do the best it can, both in examining facts and in basing judgments upon them.

Adherents of deductive ethics were alarmed some years ago by the publication of the book *Situation Ethics*.[3] Its author, the American writer J. Fletcher, caused this reaction by suggesting that certain and inflexible moral laws could on occasion be modified in view of the particular features of a given situation. His critics took fright at the element of relativity involved; for them the rules apply equally in all possible situations. Thus, it may be thought, campaigners against abortion have spoiled a good cause in the public eye by refusal to modify their principles even in the most extreme and unusual circumstances.

There was also an accusation of 'subjectivity' in the notion of 'situation ethics'. But, firstly, all moral judgments are necessarily those of a rational subject. And, secondly, all moral judgments are about particular situations. The wrong sort of subjectivity, which destroys the objectivity of moral judgment, is that which allows judgment to be weighted by considerations of personal advantage or convenience or prejudice: its reasons are not public. At the extreme, such subjectivity would judge that 'so and so is right for me because I am who I am'. And there was a flavour of this in some expositions of situation ethics, as there is in some brands of existentialism and some appeals to the primacy of individual conscience.

Moral judgment is certainly about concrete situations. For instance, if the question arises of the legitimacy of sterilization, a woman who already has five or six children is not at all in the same situation as a woman who has one or two. She may well need all the physical and spiritual energy she has to give herself properly to the existing children, and will also need the resources to foster her marriage and maintain an easy and intimate relationship with her husband.

The ideal of objectivity is the moral judgment which would be accepted by all rational persons. But that is precisely an ideal, rarely obtainable. It may be difficult to forego the certainties and sense of righteousness provided by deductive ethics, but that is often the case in our limited human and created condition. At least with the uncertainties of inductive ethics there is hope and scope for the human race to make continual advances in moral sensitivity and consensus, whereas in deductive ethics everything seems to be wrapped up once and for all. Take the case of apartheid: there is a pretty wide consensus about its evil, but a large number of presumably well-intentioned people have supported it as not only reasonable and part of the nature of things, but as Christian and the will of God. It cannot be just a matter of counting heads, or we would have an easy criterion. But at least the consensus against apartheid has triumphed and become the majority opinion among white South Africans.

We have to live with an irreducible pluralism in moral judgment simply because human beings come in such different shapes and sizes. And it is not only a matter of great public issues, like apartheid or ethnic cleansing or medical ethics in all their complexity. People just are and always will be different and judge variously about 'the good life' – what combination of worthwhile activities would make up the good life for me (Aristotle's *eudaimonia*). Not many people would see playing jazz or darts as their vocation, but who is to judge them?

Nor is morality unique in this matter of pluralism. It may at first sight seem cynical to answer Pilate's question by saying that, 'Truth is what other people think.' But this is the only criterion of objectivity in any field. Whether the light is red or green can only be judged by what 'everyone' considers to be the case. The truth of a scientific theory or discovery can only be judged by other scientists.

So with beauty in aesthetic judgment, though here there is the test of time. So with historical or any other judgment. The criterion of objectivity remains in all cases that of public reasons and public consensus.

Christian Conscience

Our conscience is *Christian* if we have been brought up in a Christian environment. We saw that as we grow up we first absorb society's values before judging them for ourselves. The Church's values are formative of our own judgment. Modern Western society may be largely agnostic, but it has been formed by centuries of Christianity and is, as it were, 'laced' with the special emphases and insights of Christianity: the value of the person, care for and love of others especially those in need, self-sacrifice, the sacredness of life, marriage as a sharing in the fidelity of God, and so on. It is noteworthy that Western countries tend to lead the way in succouring peoples in areas of flood, earthquake and famine.

But it is a *conscience*. I have to make society's values my own or modify them. I need to make my own decisions – about my way of life, political options, attitudes, and so on – and to take personal responsibility for them rather than simply follow the social herd among which I find myself. In so doing I progressively discover and create who I am.

Adolescents need a firm framework to grow on and to kick against in order to discover themselves. The framework must be firm enough to enable them to grow, but not so rigid as to strangle them. Wise parents will progressively loosen the structure and help their children increasingly to take their own responsibilities, after giving them all they can of their own tradition, wisdom and experience. It is extremely hard for young people to mature and become responsible if they receive little or no guidance, and adolescence goes on longer and longer in our present age when there are few, if any, certainties and principles maintained by adult society.

The Catholic weakness has been the opposite one of keeping the faithful immature and expecting instant, tidy and packaged answers to all moral questions: that is, answers from, and responsibility taken by, an external authority. In such a situation people are left with no responsibility for decision, for discerning right from wrong, but only for compliance.

'Discernment' is now an important and recurrent word in the literature of spirituality, especially Ignatian spirituality. It is an important element in the making of decisions, involving not only the intellectual or rational process of listing reasons for and against on both sides, but a process of standing back so as to let 'feeling' (that is, the whole person open to the action of God's Spirit) have its say.

The 'reasons of the heart' may often overturn those of the mind, revealing that the latter are narrow or pusillanimous, or based largely on self-interest or inherited prejudice. Religious communities find that, if they practise such discernment together, the process can radically alter the attitudes with which they started out. The gospel will always tend to challenge the best that human reasoning can do.

We have noted the need that is often felt for a norm against which to measure moral judgment. For Christians this norm is 'the mind of Christ', but that is not something which the Church simply possesses and hands on. Rather is it a goal towards which a pilgrim Church seeks to progress under the guidance of the Spirit, who was promised to lead the disciples into all truth. Hence the constant need for discernment. Hence, too, the fact that pastoral authority in the Church must always be attentive to the 'sense of the faithful', the prophetic voice which can speak out anywhere in the Church from the midst of concrete engagement with the many facets of human life, and can point both to new questions that human development has thrown up and to new insights into more familiar situations. In neither case are answers to be found ready-made either in scripture or tradition, that is, in Christian experience.

And the Spirit is not at work simply in the Church, let alone the Roman Catholic Church. It is highly anomalous that, while the *Decree on Ecumenism* of Vatican II recognized that 'all those justified by faith through baptism are incorporated into Christ'[4] and that . . .

> the Spirit of Christ has not refrained from using them [other Churches] as means of salvation which derive their efficacy from the fullness of grace and truth entrusted to the Catholic Church'[5]

. . . when it comes to moral questions no notice whatever is taken of the views and judgments of other Christian bodies, as if these were not relevant to the discussion. Yet it was not within the Catholic Church that the movement for the abolition of slavery, for instance, or for religious toleration, arose. But the Spirit of God has pervaded the whole world, and so the prophetic voice, challenging the Church's discernment, may be heard anywhere. The ideas of liberty, fraternity, and equality did not arise from Christian sources, nor the changing attitudes to the position of women in society. These examples show that the Church does not simply possess a complete and perfect moral doctrine, but has indeed progressed in history to greater sensitivity and insight – sometimes because of new knowledge, as in the field of psychology – and can progress further. The growth of the Kingdom is first a growth in insights, sensitiveness, attitudes, before it is an improvement in practice.

The Authority of the Church

In the sphere of human conduct, the authority of the Church can only be the authority of the Gospel – that is, reflection on the person, life, teaching, and saving work of Jesus Christ. The Gospel is not law, not simply the rule to be applied, but the challenge of an ideal which always calls the human race higher into the Kingdom however much men and women may attain. The whole thrust of the New Testament, and especially of the letters of St Paul, is that the Christian is freed from the tutelage and power of the law and driven by the power of the Spirit: he has become the slave of Christ. The Spirit impels towards love as the fulfilment of all law (*cf* Gal 5:14; Rom 13:10), and the demands of love can never be fully or perfectly met, whereas those of law can. Hence it is anomalous that the Church should have taken Jesus' prohibition of divorce as law, but the command to turn the other cheek (and so on) as Gospel: both are Gospel, and this leaves room for pastoral care of those in marital breakdown who have failed to preserve their marriage as a reality.

And the Gospel about human conduct is not moral philosophy; its sole ground is in faith. A Mother Teresa rescuing the dying from the gutters of Calcutta is not engaged in mere philanthropy: she is not doing the same action as might be a humanist engaged on the same work, for she sees and tends the suffering Christ in those she cares for. The sole authority of the Church lies in faith, not in ethics. Hence it is anomalous, even self-contradictory, if the Church delivers moral teaching that is based on human and philosophical reasoning (in an attempt to show the contents of 'right reason'): in that case the teaching carries only the authority of the controvertible reasons adduced; its voice is just one among many.

As has been noted, the Church's moral teaching conveys the emphases and insights which constitute Christian tradition. But these are open to the future and to further development and maturity. Hence there should be in the Church a constant dialectic or tension between the received and traditional on the one hand and, on the other, new insights and sensitivities that are discerned as gifts of the prophetic Spirit leading the Church into truth. Only so can the Church be an adequate sign and cause of the growth of the Kingdom on earth and in history.

Moral Law

The word 'law' is ambiguous, in that it conveys two quite distinct ideas, that of a code of rules and that of an imperative. In this chapter I have argued that moral principles normally function as rules to be kept, but are not in themselves of universal application, and that discernment is needed to decide the right course of action in cases where there are unusual factors not present in the more everyday instances from which the principle was drawn. In such cases the principle may need to be modified or even set aside for the sake of other values that are judged to be higher.

But 'moral law' also carries the idea of imperative, and both a principle and a particular decision impose such an imperative. Some people have argued that such an imperative is no more than a statement of fact and means no more than 'If you do A, B will happen' (that is, conditional rather than categorical). But the Kantian phrase 'categorical imperative' seems closer to experience. Moral facts can be described as value-laden. But we are aware of more than a value: we are conscious of an imperative, a duty. 'She is my mother, so I ought to visit her', means more than 'If I visit her, she will be pleased . . . and I will feel good.' It means I have an obligation imposed by the external fact of her motherhood, and whether I like visiting her or not.

A Good Conscience

So, a good conscience is not one that knows the rules and

can on examination say that it has kept them. A mature person has a greater responsibility than that of keeping rules laid down by authority: he or she has the responsibility of making decisions.

A good conscience is one that has taken the right means to reach a decision (and then implemented it). These means include: a gathering of the facts that is as full as possible; the marshalling of reasons pro and con as clearly and as objectively as possible; taking any relevant advice; giving full consideration to any teaching of the Church. In addition, there will be need to submit the whole process and its result to the guidance of God's Spirit, so that the whole person may be involved and the reasons of the heart may emerge. Ignatius of Loyola recommends that, with big decisions, one should offer the conclusion contentedly to God over a period of one or two months. If this brings peace of mind, then it is the right decision. That is how the will of God is discerned, and that is the sole aim of our moral search.

6

Atonement

The centre of the apostolic teaching is *resurrection* from death. Christ conquers sin and death and, raised from the dead, brings us eternal life by sending his Spirit; but is Calvary first thought of as salvific? It seems that it was Paul who first brought in this emphasis: Rom 4:25 suggests death brings about forgiveness of sin and resurrection brings salvation; this compares with Rom 6:4–11, where the imagery is of plunging into the waters of destruction.

New Testament Images

It was inevitable that Jesus' death at Passover should be interpreted in terms of *sacrifice*. It is incarnation, the sheer fact of the Word assuming our human nature, which secures atonement (at-one-ment).

John moves the supper to the day of preparation to bring this out, as Christ fulfils the type of the Passover, liberation from sin. He is the lamb of God (*cf* Jn 1:29 and Rev 7:9; see also, for the background, Is 53:7). He used the words 'cup of the new covenant in my blood', a reference to Ex 24:6 where Moses sprinkles the blood on the altar (God) and the people to ratify the covenant; and in Jn 17:19 he consecrates himself to sacrifice.

In the use of the term *ransom* the question arises: 'To whom is the price paid?' Ransom from the devil is the idea of Origen and Gregory of Nyssa: the humanity of Jesus is the bait, but the devil can't swallow the divinity! Under this imagery the ideas are conveyed of redemption, freeing from the enslavement of sin, and that Christ paid the price and that we belong to him, re-established in our Adam state.

The *physical theory*, so called from the Greek *phusis*, nature, was considered the classical theory by G. Aulen.[1]

Western theology strongly concentrates on the Passion, with agonized crucifixes (while in the East they are of a triumphant and priestly Christ) and begins to lose sight of the Resurrection as integral to Christ's saving work. Augustine's *City of God*[2] elaborates a theory of sacrifice: and introduces a distinction between real and ritual sacrifice. It is because of sin that sacrifice wears a painful aspect, the struggle to submit, for man's effective submission is broken by sin and he is incapable of real sacrifice. The latter is his interior submission to God.

Redemption (the price paid for the freeing of a slave) has the general sense of deliverance (Lk 1:68, 2:38, and 24:21; see also 1 Cor 1:30) and more specifically price (*cf* Mk 10:45; Rom 3:24; Gal 3:13).

Liberation from the slavery of law-sin-death is found in Gal 4:31 and 5:1. In 1 Cor 7:22 we are freedmen of Christ (*cf* 2 Cor 3:17 and Acts 13:39).

Expiation or propitiation (which means cleansing, with reference to the pouring of blood on the 'atonement seat' on the top of the tabernacle, and not satisfaction) is found in Rom 3:25 (*cf* 1 Jn 2:2, 4:10) and in Heb 2:17.

Reconciliation of God with mankind is found in Rom 5:10–11; 2 Cor 5:18–20; Eph 2:15–16; Col 1:19–22.

Justification by faith rather than the law is Paul's concern in Romans (misunderstood by Luther, who had scruples about salvation by works, indulgences and the like), whereas Paul is only concerned with the law of Moses (*cf* Rom 3:24–30, 4:5, 4:25). This is not the heart of Romans, or even of Paul as reformed theology has maintained.

Sanctification is the same as righteousness (being right with God) in Corinthians (*cf* 1 Cor 1:30 and 2 Cor 5:21). Christians are holy because of the in-dwelling Spirit, collective in 1 Cor 3:16, individual in 1 Cor 6:19.

The *body of Christ* is Paul's special contribution (1 Cor 6:15, 12:12; Eph 4:4).

Adoption as sons and daughters is found in Rom 9:4, 8:15, 8:23; Gal 4:5; Eph 1:5.

Transformation is the whole theme of 2 Cor 3:7–4:6 and note 3:18. Paul sees us as gazing on the face of Christ as Israel gazed on the shining face of Moses and thereby being transformed into him (*cf* John's 'we shall see him as he is', 1 Jn 3:2) both passages depending on the ancient view of optics in which the eye was thought of as an aperture into which light entered to enable sight (*cf* Mt 6:22; and see especially 2 Cor 3:18).

The Johannine themes are *eternal life* possessed now, and the *vine*; compare this with baptism and regeneration (Jn 3:5; Tit 3:5; Mt 19:28; 1 Pet 1:3; Gal 6:15).

Later Theories

With the dawn of rationalism came Anselm's famous theory of 'vicarious satisfaction',[3] which in the West then became the standard explanation.

Anselm argued that man's sin was 'quasi-infinite' and could only be put right by infinite satisfaction; but mankind could not do this, so God sent his Son whose death was of infinite value. This is a very legalistic view and is unscriptural. As we have seen, 'expiation' means cleansing, and propitiation was not thought of as a *quid pro quo*.

Abelard argued that it was only necessary for people to have faith in Christ and imitate him: this was called 'exemplarism'. But, while it covers Christians, it takes no acount of others.

Abelard's view was condemned in 1121 at the Council of Soissons.

Socinus at the time of the Reformation put forward the theory of *penal substitution*, a catch-phrase of some evangelicals: man had to be punished and so God substituted Jesus for the human race. This has a distateful view of an angry God who does not love. The legalistic Anselm saw God's love and justice, as in a law court, opposing each other, with love of course winning.

Conclusion

We may note two things.

First, the theories seem to be trying to find a mechanism to 'explain' our redemption, whereas it must remain the mystery of God's love. Second, to help our understanding there is no need to settle for only one theory: one can combine them.

So, Abelard was right within his limits.

PART TWO

Some Themes

7

Our God Reigns

Part of today's theology is to assure people that the Reign of God is not just a happy land, far far away, our heavenly home, our future fulfilment, and so on – but something that is happening all along, because God is involved in his creation (that is, what 'creating' means), and because he is more deeply involved in us and in it by the incarnation of his Son and the sending of the Son's Spirit. None of this line of thought could have been read or heard forty years ago. Religion was about the 'next life', not this one; it was other worldly (and so should be kept out of politics and firmly in church).

But how on earth can we say that sort of thing – not just that God has recently, or a couple of millenia ago, become involved in human history as such, and has been steadily building up his Kingdom and developing his Ruling or Reign – if we cannot produce any evidence of the fact. Believing is not a matter of accepting a truth against all evidence, but of seeing the signs for what they are, of seeing God at work.

And there is plenty of evidence. Let us start with racism. 'Racism' is Good News! I am not, of course, saying that racism is good news; rather, that 'racism' is part of the Good News. That needs some explanation.

But first we must note that the word usually rendered 'Kingdom' of God, for the most part means 'reign' of God in the New Testament: this is the case in Greek, the language of the New Testament, as it is in Hebrew and Aramaic – not kingdom but kingship, the activity of ruling, of being in control; not usually realm, commonwealth, political entity, but reign, sway. Jesus preached the arrival of God's reigning in the world embodied in himself. Not its perfection and completion, which is beyond and out of history (eschatological), but its definitive and irreversible establishment. From now on it would grow in human history. Jesus' parables of the Kingdom are mostly stories of growth on this earth, in this life and history: ' . . . the Kingdom of heaven [that is, of God, but Jews do not name God] is like . . . a mustard seed . . . a woman with a leaven . . . a sower sowing his seed . . . ' (Mt 13:24–33).

The earliest Christian faith was that the Risen Lord would come again: As 1 Cor 15:23–6 has it:

> Christ the first fruits, then at his coming those who belong to Christ [Christians]. Then comes the end [of history] when he delivers the kingdom to God the Father after destroying every rule and every authority and power [every demonic force harming or destroying human life which Christ conquers here on earth]. For he must reign [on earth] until he has put all his enemies under his feet [Ps 110:1 is seen as depicting the Risen Jesus sharing God's throne (Power, Spirit) with him and exercising it on earth]. The last enemy to be destroyed is death.

The above passage is universalist in the sense that it can hardly mean anything other than that Christ 'saves' all human beings – at least those in the world during his return. Even more universalist is Rom 8:19–21 where the *whole creation* is set free from the demonic forces that hold it in thrall. One must read the passage within the whole sweep of Rom 5–8, in which Christ reverses (on earth and *in history*) the destruction and death wreaked by the demonic forces (Death and Sin) let loose by Adam's disobedience.

Gerhard Lohfink has stressed[1] that:

> a) Everyone in Israel in Jesus' time believed that God would establish his kingly rule in the future. What is unique about Jesus is that he proclaimed its presence: it had arrived.

Luke should not be internalized or dissolved (Lk 17:21) into 'spirituality': it unquestionably means, 'You don't have to look all round for extraordinary signs of God's sway arriving. It is right here in your midst.' This can be compared with, 'If it is by the finger [power, spirit] of God that I cast out demons, then the kingship of God has come upon you' (Lk 11:20). Obviously, kingship and not kingdom is meant in both cases.

b) The current exegesis reads that men pray for God's rule and realm, but can do nothing to produce it. It will be brought about by God himself, when he chooses to end history. On the contrary, the parables of the rule/realm show a new People springing up, in human history, as prophesied by Jer 31:27. There can be no rule and no realm without a people acknowledging sovereignty.

c) The reign is fully present and fully given but not fully assimilated. Men and women heed, but they also resist and corrupt; weeds grow up alongside the crop. But God is in charge: the reign grows steadily, while a sower sleeps, and it can take a longish time. But it grows.

d) The building of his kingdom is, of course, God's work. But he works through men and women who, like Jesus, work the works of the one who sent them. There is no competition between God's action and man's. They are not alternatives. As Aquinas insisted, God's causality is transcendent and not to be enumerated alongside ours. God is always creator: he makes me to be me; if he acts on and through me, then my resulting action is all the more mine, all the more free.

There is recent Catholic-Reformed division on this question. No Catholic thinker believes anything other than what Lohfink so comprehensively shows is the thinking of different New Testament writers. But Protestants are inclined to subscribe to what Lohfink called 'the current exegesis'. Take, for instance, the following passage from Lesslie Newbigin :

The liberal vision of gradual progress, a vision which was present even through the first decades of the twentieth cen-

tury, has now completely faded . . . The vast majority . . .
have ceased to think hopefully about any earthly future. But
without hope action is impossible. If we are controlled by the
biblical vision, our hope for the future will be both firm and
realistic. The apocalyptic writings of the New Testament
offer a view of the future controlled by the events of the life,
death and resurrection of Jesus . . . The vision offered is not
one of gradual progress. It is of deepening conflict, of the
destruction of what seems stable, and of a final victory
beyond darkness.[2]

This is the sort of thought that confirms me in my Catholic
prejudice that Protestantism is a religion of gloom, of dark
grey, of lemonade – and sin. I well recall the privileged
occasion of my being among the first observers at a
Lambeth Conference (1968), when eventually a very wor-
ried and evangelical archbishop from Uganda got up to
complain that there had been far too little talk of sin! As a
Protestant, you have first to be a sinner, through and
through, if salvation consists in your trusting in God's forgiveness of your sins (which you can't do anything about
yourself).

You have to be a sinner – but not like those Catholics
who drink and smoke and gamble and build their churches on bingo. (Remember the film *Whisky Galore*? The
Catholics win all the way.) The good God made us to like
whisky and sex and a number of other little things, and
surely to goodness God has better things to do than to
worry about our occasional excesses, as long as they don't
do real harm to anyone. That is the opposite ethos. For a
complete Christian view one must add, of course, that God
achieves his progressive purposes and victory by working
out, in and through us, ever anew, the dying and rising of
Jesus. That is apocalyptic, as portrayed in the Book of
Revelation.

The point is this. Only God can build his reign and realm
in human life; but he does so through us (that is what the
Incarnation was and continues to be all about). He made
living beings to grow, not to start out fully mature, so he

expects kids to be kids, the way parents do.
Characteristically for the Reformed tradition 'faith' means
(as mostly in the Bible) *trust* in and hope for the future,
with reliance on God's promises and God's reliability. That
is fine. But it needs complementing or completing by the
characteristically Catholic sense of faith as 'belief that' God
is building his realm through his creatures throughout our
history. But – and this is where I began – you cannot *believe*
that God progressively reigns in history against all the evidence, or without plentiful evidence of this being the case.
Here is faith in the (characteristically Johannine) sense of
vision of the deeper realities in life and in human experience.

Of this the symbol 'racism' is one example. It is a fairly
new symbol. I was born into a, to some extent, rightly
proud colonial overseas service milieu, and was given
Kipling to read for my fourth birthday. I was a good deal
older when the idea first began to circulate that there could
possibly be negatives in the paternalistic bestowing of the
Pax Britannica on natives. (I don't think there were many
negatives, unless one wallows in much anachronism and
hindsight.) I take racism to mean the treatment by paler
men (not women or children) of darker peoples as in various ways inferior, and so reasonably, if patronizingly,
developed and organized for their own good. Of course, it
was realized that this could lead to exploitation and
oppression, but it did not necessarily do so any more than
did the *Pax Romana*.

The central factor here has, in fact, nothing to do with
colour. 'Colour', or racism as normally understood, merely
sharpens up and dramatically symbolizes what has in fact
been the whole shape of male-dominated human history,
namely the oppression of the weaker by the stronger.
Shona can oppress Matabele. Blacks in the West Indies
often maintain their domination over Indians, from West or
East, who are lighter in colour than themselves. And white-
black and black-black hostilities in South Africa are both
prominently in the news today. The British (mainly
English) have oppressed and at times practised genocide

on the Irish for centuries. The potato famine is not that long ago. And one can add other non-colour scenarios, such as American-backed internal oppression and brutality in Latin American countries, Chinese atrocities on Chinese, Arab on Arabs . . . That has been the shape of human history.

The Greeks were realists and got it right. The normal relationship between adjoining city states was war, not peace. Might, after all, is right, as the Pericles of Thucydides so plausibly argued in the course of the Melian Debate (about whether to exterminate the entire population of Melos). This is how Athens laid the foundations of European civilization. So you declared peace for 20 or 30 years – longer would be unrealistic – and kept it or not as seemed advantageous. But it was the men who took these decisions and who did the fighting; and it seemed they could only be controlled by their women when the latter went on strike (so the *Lysistrata* of Aristophanes).

What I am saying, then, is that the newish word 'racism' stands for the very recent awareness that there is something wrong with all this . . . Not merely that we can only survive, if we all respect persons as persons, irrespective of colour and so on; but that men have been consistently sub-human throughout their history. This new awareness is a big step forward. We are slowly getting to grips with the fact that, as David Jenkins wrote ' . . . no one can be fully human until everyone is fully human'.[3] And it works both ways:

> . . . the discovery by peoples, classes and races who have hitherto been dependent and made use of for the power, consumption and enjoyment of a limited class of their fellows that they are oppressed and exploited is an essential step in the discovery of their own humanness.[4]

I would only add that we do not emerge on this earth as fully constituted persons. We only become persons by progressively extending and deepening our relations with other persons: and obviously we must have total width-

and-depth relations to all the persons there are, let alone those who have been and will be, before we can be fully persons. Only the God who revealed himself as the inter-personal Father-Son-Spirit can do that.

Only in God shall we be fully persons. Conversely, a good way of putting the doctrine of the Incarnation is to say that it takes God to be fully human.

And to what I have said about racism must be added awareness of unjust economic structures (structural sin), pollution of the environment and erosion of the world's resources. We could look again at Romans to recapture the vision of how we are bound together with each other and with all creation in a longing for, but confident hope of, being set free in the fullness of Christ's kingdom (Rom 8). One might even say that the author of Col 1:13–20 was hardly going beyond Paul's Romans in interpreting the body of Christ as the cosmos. The so-called 'developed nations' have lost that sense of oneness with the natural living and immaterial creation which remains strong in 'less developed' peoples, in Celtic spirituality and in Eastern and African religions.

And it is not just worldwide matters. Since I was a boy there has been far more effort to care for the unemployed, for the physically and mentally handicapped. We no longer speak of 'lunatic asylums', but try to respect the humanity and dignity of all. There is continued effort to create conditions of personal growth for prisoners and awareness of shortcomings. We do not hang convicted murderers any more – and there is no calling back the Birmingham Six once they have been hanged. Indeed, prison used not to be a form of punishment but a way of getting people to pay their debts (*cf* Charles Dickens's *Little Dorrit*). It is not long since people were hanged or deported to Australia for stealing a sheep; Islamic law cuts the hands off thieves – a far cheaper method. It is precisely our increasing humanity towards offenders (who may well be victims of an unjust social and economic order) that has produced all the problems of custodial punishment. We 'play God' with other people a bit less as time goes on.

Perhaps above all other contemporary awarenesses that are Good News is that of male chauvinism and the process of what might be called the greening of women to which it has led. This is more than giving women the fullest opportunities for making their own (feminine) contributions to human life, because that could still mean 'human life as devised and run by men'. It stands out most clearly from the other areas of awareness we have been considering that it is women's best attitudes to other tribes, races, social groups, that need to play at least an equal part in the structuring of society nationally and internationally: negatively, the aversion from physical violence of those whose lot brings them enough pain already; and positively the gentle and civilizing touch.

So we have no need to whistle in the dark about God being in control of history, that is, his whole creation. That would suggest a false (Enlightenment) view of faith as a leap in the dark or into the future. Nor do we need simply to rely on God's faithfulness to his promises, his fidelity whatever our own infidelity. Our faith can, rather, be a Johannine leap into the light as we see the meaning of observable facts.

One could plausibly construct a historical argument as follows: the wheel proved to be a very dangerous invention; indeed, every advance in scientific knowledge has brought new dangers and problems while overcoming old ones. But as the human race has hitherto solved its problems, there are good grounds for thinking it will solve those of the present – over-population, erosion of resources, nuclear threat, warming up of the planet, or any others. Such an argument could possibly establish a probability, though one would have to note that the choices confronting mankind seem to get increasingly apocalyptic, even while the opportunities become ever more wonderful, and feel it remains rather a toss-up.

There is less and less room for making mistakes (Chernobyls could multiply . . .).

Only faith as a personal encounter with the living God in our contemporary human world can produce certainty of quite a different order: God reigns. How could he not? And for a Christian this confident expectation is clinched by a further fact: the victory of God's Christ does not hang in the balance of human choices. It is already won.

First Corinthians

The epistle was written during Paul's stay in Ephesus, probably in the early spring of 57. It divides easily into three sections followed by a conclusion.[1]

The three sections comprise: an introduction and thanksgiving; news from Corinth with a letter from Chloe[2]; and a letter raising various points.

Address and Thanksgiving

An Introduction (1 Cor 1:1–9)

1:1   Paul claims to be a divinely appointed apostle, not a missionary sent by men. Sosthenes is probably the man of Acts 18:17, the ruler of the synagogue at Corinth beaten by the Jews. The church is the assembly of those chosen by God (saints) and therefore 'holy'.

1:5   'Word' includes speech of every kind, including tongues, and points forward to some of their gifts.

News from Corinth

On Wisdom and Division at Corinth (1 Cor 1:10 to 6:20)

1:12   Apollos, after instruction by Priscilla and Aquila, visited Corinth: he is an Alexandrian and learned (possibly the author of Hebrews), and so may have started the discussion about wisdom (*cf* Acts 18:24 to 19:1). 'I belong to

Christ,' seems rather odd, so should be taken as Paul's answer to their arguments.

1:13   Baptism was into the name of Jesus, the Trinitarian formula being later. In his criticism of 'wisdom' Paul is not thinking of the great philosophers but of sophists of the Gnostic type: Greeks look to knowledge, Jews to miracles as signs of God's power, but Paul demands faith: 'We preach a crucified Messiah.' This is about the only place Paul uses Christ as a title as it is normally simply a surname; the messianic hopes of the Jews would mean nothing in his Hellenistic churches.

1:30   This refers to the Wisdom literature of the Old Testament and is evidence of an early wisdom Christology in the New Testament.

2:5   Rhetoric produces intellectual conviction: manifestation of the Spirit's power produces faith.

2:6   The rulers are the demons behind the actual thrones (see 2:8), the elemental astral powers who operate through the civil rulers.

2:7   God's secret wisdom means the plan that is now out and is a secret no longer. In 2:8, the Gnostic language recalls the myth of the Redeemer unrecognized in his descent on earth. The point in 2:9 is that human faculties are incapable of penetrating the divine plan. It is for God to reveal it, and he does so to those who love, not those who 'know'.

2:13   The origin of the phrase 'discernment of spirits'.

3:15   The person is saved 'as a brand from the burning'. The use of the passage as evidence of belief in purgatory is wide of the mark.

3:16   Paul twice uses 'you are God's temple': first, here, the community is in mind; and, in 6:19, the individual. They replace the Jerusalem temple.

3:22   'You are Christ's and so liberated from all human masters.'

4:1   This determines your attitude to Paul, Cephas and the like. (The attempt to construct a division between Paul and Peter on the basis of this verse and the Galatians dispute is quite unfounded.)

4:6   The text is untranslatable, as a scribal marginal comment has been written into it, so omit 'not to go beyond what is written'.

4:9   'God has paraded us like the last exhibits in the arena.'

On Immorality (1 Cor 5:1–13)

5:1   The case must concern the dead father's second wife: such incest is forbidden 'even' in Roman law. It appears that the freedom boasted of (*cf* 6:12 and 10:23) has led to moral laxity.

5:4   Paul calls a spiritual assembly with them to excommunicate the man. So some sort of exorcism is envisaged, and this will inevitably have physical effects. Once out of the Body he will be liable to disease and death, for he will be thrust back into the power of Satan.

5:6   The same proverb is used in Gal 5:9, all leaven had to be removed from the house for the Passover. The Christians are the true unleavened bread, Passover bread being unleavened. Their Paschal lamb is Christ, indeed they are the one bread of Christ, his Body. 'Sacrifice the Passover' was the technical term for killing the lamb.

5:8   'Sincerity and truthfulness', a clear conscience; as things are they are hypocritical in conniving at the incest.

On Litigation (1 Cor 6:1–11)

6:1   The 'unrighteous' are unbelievers; not a slur on the Roman legal system, but a protest against taking cases to non-Christians. That God's people will judge the world is found in apocalyptic.

On the Root of the Trouble (1 Cor 6:12–20)

6:12   Here Paul is dealing with a Gnostic and dualist type of thinking (the Gnostic heresy is centuries later), which maintains that nothing bodily is of relevance to the life of the spirit, and hence rejects resurrection. 'All things are lawful for me', is a slogan at Corinth, and the repetitions should be understood as Paul replying. 'The lord is for the body' is a very striking remark: in this context of eating there must be a reference to the Eucharist, as Paul always uses 'Lord' for the risen Christ: communion prepares our resurrection.

6:15   Prostitutes would have been pagan temple prostitutes, thought to put one in communion with the god. Body and spirit are two opposing worlds and I am able to give myself to either. In 6:20, 'You were bought in the slave market at a price' and then set free by your owner (*cf* Gal 3:13, 4:5; and Rom 3:24).

A Letter from Corinth

On Marriage and Related Questions (1 Cor 7:1–40)

7:1   There is a natural transition from body-thought to marriage questions. It becomes clear (*cf* 7:29–31) that Paul's advice is given in the understanding that the world is about to end, and so any construction of a permanent doctrine of marriage is quite misplaced.

7:4   The equality and parallelism is a Christian idea – though Paul is not a raging egalitarian! The concession is either the periods of abstinence, or the verse refers to all from 7:2 on; the latter seems likely in view of the next verse – Paul is not ordering them to marry.

7:10   One of the very few references in Paul to Jesus' teaching, which confirms the Mark version of the saying of Jesus prohibiting divorce (Mk 10:2–12).

7:14   It is striking that there is no mention of baptism. Paul regards the child of a Christian parent as already in the Body, and the obvious inference is that there is then no need to baptize. This rather pulls the rug from under the infant baptism controversy, for if children were not baptized in infancy, there is no evidence that they were baptized later: it is an argument from silence but a somewhat noisy one!

7:15   All the verse says is that the Christian should not leave the non-Christian, but the non-Christian may separate if he wishes. He does not say that the Christian may marry again, so the so-called 'Pauline privilege' has no basis here!

7:16   The implication is that by living the marriage the Christian will save the other (bodily union again).

7:21   This does not mean 'use the chance to become free': throughout the passage, Paul's advice is that they should stay in the state in which they were called (became Christians). The freed slave was not a free man but a 'freedman', owing loyalty to the master who had freed him.

7:32   Paul gives the same advice of stability to the unmarried boys and girls who are engaged.

7:31   Here is the proof that Paul writes in imminent expectation of the End.

On Food Sacrificed to Idols (1 Cor 8:1 to 11:1)

8:1   The meat in the market would probably have been sacrificed to idols, there being no butchers' shops in our sense. The convert Jews would have scruples about slaughtering and the gentiles had cast idolatry aside, so both could have scruples.

8:2   'He sets himself up as enlightened.' Using the 'weak and the strong', Paul means what we would mean by conservatives and progressives: one realizes he is free to eat, but another has scruples.

8:10   Many pagans no longer attached meaning to these rituals but attended them as social functions. Paul's advice is the same as John's: don't decide according to your view, but with an eye to what might trouble your fellow Christian. That is, love.

9   There appears to be an abrupt break, and some

opinion suggests that we have a passage here from another letter. But we all break off when writing a letter and put in a parenthesis. 'Am I not an apostle? Have I not seen the Lord?' Clearly, some at Corinth were questioning whether Paul, not one of the twelve, was a true apostle (*cf* the factions in 1:10). Paul's reply shows that he thought two things were needed for a true apostle: to have seen the risen Lord and to have been commisioned by him, and not by men.

10:1   Paul returns to the subject of idol meats. Baptism was a plunging and not a pouring, so they are baptized into Jesus (once more, the name of Jesus was used, the Trinitarian formula being later).

10:3   Verse 3 speaks of 'spiritual' food and is the basis for our offertory prayers. Moses struck the rock at Meriba, but the Israelites moved on, so there was a rabbinic gloss that the rock followed them.

10:7   The reference is to pagan feasts, possibly with some reference to the Eucharist and to Num 25:1–4 where the people sat down to idolatrous meals, and rose to lewd revels.

10:11   'What happened to them was . . . ': Paul sees the past events as having the force of 'types' for Christians. The 'ends of the ages' means the end of one age and the start of the next.

10:16   The third and concluding cup of the Passover meal is called the cup of blessing/thanksgiving.

10:17   There are various ways of understanding the verse, the most likely being 'because there is one loaf, we are one body'. That is, the chief effect of the Eucharist is the unity of the Church.

10:18   'Consider the historic Israel', as opposed to the spiritual Israel, the Church. The idea of an offering in the temple was that of a meal shared with God; the altar is his table, and one either gives him the lot (holocaust) or shares with him, taking home a half (the priests were entitled to God's share). It is clear that Paul regards the Eucharist as sacrificial. There used to be a discussion, 'Is it a meal or a sacrifice?', but all sacrifices are meals. If you sacrificed to an idol, you were sharing a meal with him.

10:19 What am I saying, that the offering has real meaning? No, rather, that they are sacrificing to real demons, not to God.

10:22 The verse is addressed to the 'strong'. 'Are we to defy God? Are we stronger than he?'

On the Christian Assembly (1 Cor 11:2–34)

11:3 In 8:6 Christ is the pattern of the creation of the male.

11:4 The Old Testament 'head' is used for 'ruler'. No one seems to know when male Jews started praying with their hats on.

11:10 'Because of the angels', that is wicked angels. In Gen 6:4 there is embedded a pagan legend of the Watchers who lusted after the fair daughters of men and united with them – one of the Old Testament explanations of the origins of evil.

The whole passage reads like the reply of any religious superior: worse arguments are heaped on bad, and the last resource is, 'In any case it is not our custom.'!

11:23 Paul refers to what he learnt (why 'from the Lord'?) after his conversion, so here we have the oldest tradition.

11:24 ' . . . which is for you?' The manuscripts vary showing that each Church had slightly different formulas.

11:26 These are Paul's words, not those of Jesus. By 'Lord' he means the risen One, so we do not eat the mortal body: he holds together death and resurrection. Much mediaeval controversy rested on the rather crude interpretations of the time.

It is necessary to realize that Paul does not think as a Greek, for whom body and soul are separate entities: for him they represent wholes of experience. We experience ourselves as bodies, flesh-bodies, subject to moral and physical ills, but also as spirit-bodies (a contradiction to a Greek), open to the action of God, so the body we receive is the spirit-body of Christ.

11:29   This does not mean, by 'judgment', that God will be displeased, but that the person will suffer physical ills.

The Eucharist was regarded as 'the medicine of immortality', saving one from illness and death.

On Spiritual Gifts (1 Cor 12:1 to 14:40)

12:3   No one ever says, 'Jesus be cursed!' Why should a Christian say this? The explanation is to be found in Deut 21:23: ' . . . cursed be everyone that hangs on a tree'. Jesus incurred the curse by his crucifixion, but he did not remain 'anathema' (Gal 3:13) but rose again. So a Christian who says this is denying the Resurrection.

12:4   'Varieties of gifts': charismatics usually appeal to these chapters as the basis of speaking in tongues and indeed at Vatican II Cardinal Suenens's famous speech, showing that the gifts (Greek *charisma*) were not of an extraordinary nature, but embraced everyday services/ministries such as administration, made the word common parlance. But it becomes clear that Paul is here *downgrading* tongues, whether these are foreign languages or baby talk. They come last each time and other gifts are preferred. He was probably a bit 'high' when he first evangelized Corinth and gave too much prominence to tongues; so here he is putting matters straight.

12:8   The difference between wisdom and knowledge is that shown in moral and doctrinal matters.

12:9   All have faith in the ordinary sense; what is meant is trust in their power to work wonders in Christ's name.

12:28   In the list of ministries here and elsewhere (*cf* Rom 12), which are not of course meant to be exhaustive, apostles always come first, and then prophets. Prophecy does not mean prediction, but in general the power to speak in a way that goes to the heart. Teachers come third: they would instruct children and converts.

13   There follows the famous 'hymn' to love. One might wonder why faith persists in heaven, but as before it is trust that is meant – God will fulfil all he has promised.

It is likely that the 'noisy gong and clanging cymbal' of 13:1 refers to pagan worship, and is one more 'swipe' at tongues!

14:22 It appears that non-Christians could come to the assembly, but only for the liturgy of the word: they would be excluded from the Eucharist.

On the Resurrection (1 Cor 15:1-58)

15:3 Here we have the earliest version of the kerygma, what Paul was taught and what he preached. C. H. Dodd wrote a famous book in which he asked 'What Scriptures?'[3] That is, what passages from the Old Testament are found quoted everywhere and so were the common pool of proof-texts used by the apostles and others? Dodd then showed that all basic Christian doctrine is contained in them.

15:4 'That he was buried.' Paul does not mention the empty tomb, but he always uses the word 'resurrection' (not exaltation, and so on); this conjures up the picture of a man sitting up and walking out. The appearance to Peter is given in Lk 24:34 only, and that to James (the brother of the Lord, not one of the apostles) is only found here. Scholars think that the primitive kerygma ends here, and that the sentences beginning 'Then' are Paul's addition.

15:12 It is clear that some at Corinth were denying the Resurrection, for to a Greek the idea was incomprehensible: the real person was the soul which at death left behind this rather regrettable appendage, an idea which had a profound effect on Christian spirituality.

15:25 This verse gave rise to milleniarism, the belief that Christ would reign on earth for a thousand years. The 'last enemy' means the demonic power that holds the world in thrall (*cf* Rom 5 where there is the same contrast between Christ and Adam).

15:29 Evidence for vicarious baptism of those under instruction who had died before being received.

15:40 God gives the risen person a spirit-body. 'Star differs from star': they were thought to be made of different kinds of celestial matter.

15:44   The Greek says, not 'physical' but 'psychical'. The reference in 15:46 has a rabbinic gloss on Genesis, saying Adam (the heavenly man) came first and then the present race after the fall.

15:53   Here it is shown clearly that Paul did not hold the notion of natural immortality: our only hope of survival lies in the resurrection of Christ.

15:56   The picture is of a scorpion: the sting is the demonic sin, the law is the muscle that sticks it in.

16:22   Paul uses the Aramaic word *maranatha*, used in the Eucharist.[4] 'Let him be accursed' was the sign for the non-believers to leave the assembly.

Your Children Are Holy

'Otherwise your children would be unclean, but as it is they are holy.' (1 Cor 7:14). This latter verse of St Paul affords me special glee and fascination, because of its obvious implication and its undercutting of controversy.

Paul is here dealing with a set of questions sent to him from Corinth. One set sent by Chloe has questions about marriage – and what a meal the Church has made of Paul's answers in the course of history!

No one seems to think themselves into the actual situation which Paul is addressing; even if they know about it in another part of their mind, their imagination at this point seems to go dormant. At the time, 'the Lord' (a phrase which to Paul always means the risen Jesus) was coming any day. So, is it all right for engaged couples to marry? Or should they stay engaged? To all such questions Paul replies: 'My advice is that it is better to remain in the state of life you were in when you were called by God [that is, became Christians]. But there is no compulsion about it. Feel free.'

Among the questions there was one about a Christian married to a non-Christian, and Paul gives the same advice, but adds:

> If you stay together, your partner will be saved, otherwise not . . . And what about your children? As it is, they are 'holy', but they too will be lost if you leave them to the other partner(1 Cor 7:14).

The first 'nonsense' to be made out of this passage has been to base on it the so-called 'Pauline privilege', the right of a

Christian to a second marriage to another Christian, if the first marriage to a non-Christian breaks up. This is something Paul never dreamt of. He says nothing whatever about another marriage, and this would be in flat contradiction to his repeated advice to stay as you were when the Lord called you, as he is coming soon.

A mix-up has also gone on in Christianity about infant baptism. Baptists and others say it was not the practice in New Testament times and so is illegitimate: baptism requires the faith of the person to be baptized. Catholics counter by saying that Paul baptized whole households, and some must have had infants, even if no specific mention is made of them. A weak argument from silence. Meanwhile, both sides overlook that the only question that has ever arisen in the Church has been about the baptism of the *children of Christian parents*. So, whether there were or were not infants among the Jewish or pagan households mentioned is irrevelant. Rather must we ask, did Paul think that the children of Christian parents *needed* baptising at all?

It is in fact obvious from 1 Cor 7:14, that he did not. Paul says:

> For the non-Christian partner is sanctified by the Christian one; otherwise your children would be 'unclean', but as it is they are 'holy'.

Now, 'holy' is precisely one of the titles Paul uses for Christians. The 'holy ones' are holy, because God is holy and *he* has called and chosen them: nothing to do with holiness in any 'virtuous' sense. So the greeting at the beginning of the letter should run: 'Paul, an apostle of Jesus Christ by God's will, and Sosthenes your fellow Christian [brother]: to God's community at Corinth, people consecrated in Christ, holy because called by God [or 'chosen'] like me . . . '

Paul has a very simple 'body theology' (of which more later) running right through the letter. Hence there can be no doubt at all that he thought:

(a) that the non-Christian spouse was 'in' the Body of Christ, precisely by being *bodily* united to the Christian (and it is odd that the Catholic tradition which has insisted on the sacredness of sexual union in marriage, and considered the latter a sacrament, should never have seen it): hence, the non-Christian is saved while joined to the Christian, but otherwise 'out' of the Body of Christ and so lost; and

(b) the child is literally from the body of the Christian parent, and so 'in', as long as he or she is not taken off by the non-Christian. There is no evidence at all of any children of such parents being baptized as infants until long after the time of the New Testament. Still less is there evidence of their being baptized at a later age.

So, rather than 'fudge' what New Testament authors are saying, because of preconceived ideas of doctrine to which they must conform, we must allow the evidence to challenge our doctrinal ideas.

In the course of history, and of the development of the scholastic doctrine of baptism, two things happened to the sacraments: they were over-separated from each other and regarded as producing quite different effects (so that it could, for example, be forgotten that, as the Council of Trent says, Holy Communion forgives sins); and they were separated off from the living reality in which they are embedded, the community Church.

A modern theology approaches sacraments from an understanding of the Church as the believing community in which the risen Lord dwells by the gifts of his life, and in which he acts. Before the rise of scholasticism, Augustine, in arguing for the validity of baptism by a sinful priest, had insisted: 'When Peter baptizes, it is Christ who baptizes; when Judas baptizes, it is Christ who baptizes.' So the sacraments must be thought of as a particular ritual occasion when the Church crystallizes or embodies, and conveys or offers *what she is* and *what Christ is doing in her* all the time.

So we have to entertain the idea that the child of

Christian parents is not born 'in the power of the devil' – as pagans could be thought to be, a horrible idea, reinforced by the long use for infants of the rite for baptizing adult pagans, wth its graphic imagery of their rescue from a sinful world – but *born in the Church.*

If we entertain this idea, two large areas of rethinking are needed: first, what we might mean by original sin; second, what the effect of baptism is.

The first area would require an extensive re-treatment of the whole bundle of ideas that goes under the umbrella 'original sin'. Here I will only say that it needs to be seen as a half-truth, which can be very distorting if regarded as the whole truth. From Augustine onwards there was the underlying conviction that 'outside the Church there is no grace of Christ'; but a long development of theology reached its climax at Vatican II, with its assertion that the grace of Christ reaches all men, whether they know it or not – God addresses and offers himself to all. Hence, we are all born, not only with limited and flawed human equipment, destined in any case to mature and grow; but also, with varying degrees of explicit awareness, in the grace of Christ.

Second, what then, in such a view, is the effect of baptism? It would follow, both for a child of Christian parents and in all other cases, that baptism is a *sign* of what the Church is and does. It becomes possible to assert that the rite of baptizing can be thought of in itself, and in abstraction from the Church which performs it, as simply a sign. It is the Church which produces the effect. And it is no longer necessary to think of the effect(s) of baptism being produced then and there, in a flash, as we may have been used to thinking. (I once heard of a parish across the Atlantic where technology had been added to the traditional symbols; a purple spotlight shone on the font until the water and the words, whereupon the infant turned white!)

The 'sense of the faithful' today no longer feels that the child must be baptized immediately, even before the mother is on her feet again, so that the godmother is expected to be holding the baby: the revised rite of baptism has the mother doing that. The whole idea of an 'instant effect' of the ritual has long been thought to be somewhat magical and superstitious – not fitting in at all with the personal relations between God, the parents, the Christian community and the child. But, if we think through the idea that baptism is a sign of what the Church is and does a number of things follow.

The first conclusion must be: only to the extent that the parents *are* 'Church', are committed and practising Christians, can baptism be effective in the course of time. The child is born into the Church, is 'holy'. And the participation of the believing community, as well as the presence and involvement of godparents and families, demonstrate that all the resources of Christ's Body will be there to nourish the growth of the life which God has given already. A baptism is the occasion when a small baby, hitherto belonging solely to the immediate family, is welcomed by the broader society of families and friends, and by the local Christian community as a whole: hence the pressure for baptism during Sunday Mass.

A further conclusion along the same lines is that the 'point' of baptizing an infant in danger of death is, not so much to do something essential for the child, as to do something essential for the parents: to demonstrate to and reassure them of the love of Christ, which already enfolds their infant, which will be particularly important if the baby dies.

In this connection we should not underestimate the role of the Christian mother in conveying the reality of God's love, God's prevenient and spontaneous love, to her child. If faith is to be understood (as it should be) as a personal human response to the self-giving love of God which comes to us and addresses us in each other as members of Christ's Body, then, not only does the mother have the first and fundamental role to play in mediating to her child the eternal love of God, which beats through her own, but, in considering the genesis and gradual growth of faith (the effect of baptism) in any child of a Christian mother, we cannot leave out of consideration the mother's constant nurture and care of the new member of the family from the time of conception onwards. It is, incidentally, interesting that canon law takes the position that, if a baby is baptized in hospital in an emergency, then the Church to which the child belongs is not that of the baptizing minister but that of the parents' intention.

Conversely, one has to have the hardihood to say that, in an absolute or extreme case where the parents are in *no* sense 'Church', but merely ask to 'have baby done' so as to follow socially accepted ritual, or not offend grandparents, then the rite of baptism effects precisely nothing. This seems to be recognized by the Church's prohibition of baptism unless there is some possibility, however tenuous, of the child being given a Christian upbringing. It is a difficult pastoral question facing all traditions which follow the century-old practice of infant baptism. The fact that the parents came along at all suggests that there is something there which can and should be encouraged, a flickering flame to be fanned rather than extinguished. But it is a pastoral question and does not alter one's doctrinal position.

Paul had perhaps not fully thought out his own position in 'systematic' terms. But his view that the child would be saved if united to the Christian parent, and lost if separated, seems to confirm the notion that it is the Church, the community of faith and explicit Christian life, which brings about the effects, and that the rite of baptizing is in itself a sign of this which the Church is and does.

I would ask, in addition, for serious consideration of the beginnings of faith in an infant (even unborn) as response to the mother's love. Our faith has to have a beginning – and does it ever become perfect? Perhaps paedobaptists and their opponents agree after all: faith in the recipient is necessary for baptism!

Body Theology

A great difficulty in understanding the New Testament is that the whole of it originated from people who 'thought' Jewish while they wrote in Greek, the common language of the Eastern Roman Empire (that is, east of Italy).

Greek was a second language to all of them, however well they knew Greek philosophical ideas. The Hellenist Greeks had been in charge in Palestine since Alexander the Great, and any educated person like Paul would have been only too painfully aware of Greek thought. As a good Pharisee he would have resisted its possible corruption of Jewish religious thought might and main. The modern translators, such as those of today's Bible at least sound like someone writing a letter, though there is nothing high-flown about the RSV.[1]

The extraordinary thing about the Jews of Jesus' time was that their entire culture, including thought-forms and language, arose from one 'book', the Old Testament. They had no language at all which was not religious in origin; hence the appalling difficulty of understanding what a Jew is *saying when writing* in Greek, *every* key-word having to be translated back from the Greek language to its Jewish religious meaning.

Our own century has been the first to have the tools to do this job. So, no blame to earlier generations for sometimes having got themselves into paroxysms of theological dispute over matters which can now be understood quite differently.

The word 'body' is a prime instance. As we all know, the Greek mind-set is to distinguish A from B: A and B are mutually exclusive. So 'body' is other than soul (life-source or principle) and 'soul' is other than body. This led to the great Greek advances in mathematics and in medical and other natural sciences, which were lost until the last century. The Jew, on the contrary, always thought in, what are best described as, 'wholes of experience'[2] – that is in terms of human experience, and indeed, of man's relation to God. I experience my *self* as a body – well, I do, don't I? That 'self' is the right translation for *soma*, body: the experienced 'me'. The 'I' which does the experiencing is *psyche*, conscious life, or centre of consciousness. I experience my body-self as fragile and liable to physical and moral sickness, and this is what is meant by 'flesh'; and I also experience my body-self as spirit, *pneuma*, namely, open to the creative action of God.

'God is spirit' and able to transform me by degrees into sharing his own specific spirit-life (two words for the same reality, as 'spirit'=breath=life-principle). This, incidentally, explains 'This is my body', and all New Testament theology.[3] One must be clear that this body-self is not the 'I' who do the experiencing, but the 'me' that I experience (or, in philosophical jargon, the object of reflex consciousness and not the subject of immediate or direct consciousness).

Well, Paul has a body-theology running right through his letters to Corinth. It is his version of John's doctrine of incarnation, only John used 'flesh' to stress that the Word really became a frail mortal man, experiencing life the way we do, with all its uncertainties and insecurities: he was not a baby who knew all about astrophysics and held out on St Joseph on the subject of carpentry. (The Church has tended to misread 'flesh' in other terms.)

At the Last Supper, Jesus spoke in the parallelisms of Jewish poetic diction: this is my body-self broken (or given) for you; this is my life poured out for you. The blood is the vehicle of life, which is the reason why Jews were forbidden in Leviticus to consume meat with the blood in it; life is God's life. No Jew would make the sort of Greek-spun distinction between created and uncreated life as a hard-and-fast dichotomy. So spirit (breath)=blood (life)='soul'.

All are symbols of the most magical and wonderful of our experiences – being alive!

So Paul's comparison with a body when he is explaining our union with the risen Lord was meant not only to say we were one being, or even one person, with him, but to end the squabbles at Corinth by showing that different gifts (*charismata*) of the Spirit were not meant to put people at odds with each other, but to enrich the life of the community. The Spirit creates diversity for the sake of unity – as in marriage.

But it would be a mistake to think that Paul's picture of the believing Christian community as Christ's Body is simply the use of a fairly common Stoic metaphor for the body politic being 'like' a human body. He has to struggle to find language to express the inexpressible: the relation of Christians to their risen Lord. But he means something extremely realist by this relation, as I will now try to bring out.

First and foremost, he struggles to find words to convey the 'risen-ness' of the Lord himself. Among his converts at Corinth were those who believed that Christ was risen, but did not believe in resurrection for themselves. The most convincing explanation for this, to us strange, situation is that when Paul first preached the Good News at Corinth, he expected the Lord to come again so soon that the question of believing Christians dying had simply not arisen, and so nothing had been said about *their* resurrection from the dead: they would all be alive at the Lord's coming. But since those times, some seven years previously, some Christians had died and this gave rise to a series of problems. Paul had to reply that, whether dead or alive at Christ's Coming, all Christians would need 'transforming' (1 Cor 15:51–3) into a risen state. One of the difficulties was that converts from Hellenism at Corinth would have inherited with their culture a rigid distinction between body and soul, and would favour a doctrine of immortality of the soul, despising any idea of resurrection of the body (as at Athens in Acts 17). In reply, Paul forces them to think in terms of the resurrection of human beings and openly rejects any idea of a natural immortality of the soul. Man's sole hope of survival lies in sharing in the Resurrection of Christ: 'If Christ has not been raised . . . then those Christians who have died have perished' (1 Cor 15:17–18); and ' . . . this perishable nature must put on the imperishable, and this mortal nature must put on immortality' (1 Cor 15:53). It does not possess it already.

Behind this argument lies the conviction that Jesus himself, who as true man experienced himself as flesh-body-self, was raised by the power of God to be spirit-body-self. The Corinthians must not have too materialistic ideas of resurrection, as if this flesh-self were raised as such: 'I tell you this, brothers: flesh and blood cannot inherit the kingdom of God, nor does the perishable inherit the imperishable' (1 Cor 15:50); the first man (Adam means 'man') became a living being; the last Adam (Christ) became a life-giving spirit (1 Cor 15:45). So Jesus in his Resurrection has ceased to be flesh-body-self and has become spirit-body-self, indeed has become Spirit in fullness, giving God's life to others. We must be transformed into him and so become spirit-body-selves 'in Christ'. The realism is very strong. It is possible that Paul's most realistic passage about Christ's risenness is to be found in 2 Corinthians, where he appears to say: 'Now, the Lord is Spirit' (2 Cor 3:17), but the exact meaning is open to dispute. However, other passages show the realism intended in Paul's quasi-identification of the Christian with the risen Christ, notably in Galatians: 'You are all one personal being in Christ' (Gal 3:28), where the Greek says, 'You are all *heis*' which is the masculine for 'one' and so denotes a personal being; the neuter would have denoted more vaguely 'one reality'.

But the transformation which the Christian undergoes is not something which simply happens when we die. As is always the perspective in New Testament eschatology, it is a case of 'already so, but not yet fully so'. We have already been plunged in baptism into the death of Christ, and have risen into his risenness (*cf* Rom 6:3–11, where the tension between what is already the case and what is still to be accomplished is maintained). 'By [or in] one Spirit we were all baptized into one body' (1 Cor 12:13): that this is the Body of Christ is made clear a few verses later: 'Now you are the Body of Christ and individually members of him' (1 Cor 12:27).

The realism of Paul's body-theology comes out strongly in the passages where he deals with cases of immorality reported from Corinth. There is, first, the case of the man who is living with his dead father's second wife (not his own mother), something forbidden as incest 'even among the pagans' (1 Cor 5:1), that is in Roman law. Paul summons a sort of spiritual assembly (in his absence) with the Christian community to excommunicate the offender; that is, to cut him off from 'the Body'. It is obviously expected that the offender will then suffer physical effects, even death: he is thrust back into the power of Satan 'for the destruction of the flesh' (1 Cor 5:5), but so that his spirit may be saved on the day of the Lord's coming, for he remains a baptized Christian.

Later, in the context of dealing with sexual immorality in general, Paul strikes at the root of the trouble at Corinth: a dualist type of thinking, which maintains that nothing bodily is of relevance to the life of the spirit, and which consequently rejects resurrection of the body. It leads some to excesses in food and drink, but also to sexual immorality. Paul replies: 'The body is not meant for immorality but for the Lord.'

As always, by 'the Lord' Paul means the risen Christ, who does not cease to be man by being raised, but is now Spirit-body-self and not flesh-body-self. He then adds the most striking, even astonishing, complement: ' . . . and the Lord is for the body' (1 Cor 6:13). It is possible, as he has just been talking about eating and drinking, that Paul has the Eucharist at least at the back of his mind: we receive in Holy Communion the Spirit-self of the risen Jesus to transform us more and more into him. But the immediate question is that of sexual morality. We are *not* to despise our bodies, as a dualist view, and indeed all too often a Christian spirituality infected by Platonism, would suggest. Not only are our bodily selves 'for the Lord', and therefore holy; but the risen Lord is 'for' our body-self: he is raised to save us, to incorporate or include us in his Spirit-body-self (1 Cor 6:14). So Paul can go on:

> Surely you know [that is, didn't I tell you before?] that your bodies are members of Christ. Shall I therefore take the members of Christ and make them members of a prostitute? Your body is a temple of the Holy Spirit within you, which [Spirit] you have from God (1 Cor 6:15–19).

There is no mere metaphor here. Our bodily union in illegitimate sex is a bodily union forced on Christ. The lesson is all the more pointed in that, at Corinth, prostitutes would be temple prostitutes, and intercourse with them would be understood as bodily union with the pagan god. But conversely, as we have seen, sexual union in marriage is sanctifying: it can even draw the non-Christian partner into Christ by bodily union.

It is well known that not only Judaism but the Christianity of the East also have been free from the hang-ups about sex which have bedevilled Western Christianity. But Paul's thinking suggests a good deal more than the negative encouragement to be free from hang-ups – more than the perhaps cold and austere recommendation that we should 'respect' our bodies. Surely, we should venerate and love them as vehicles of our transforming union with 'the Lord'. God made us as we are, made us with various bodily functions. In themselves they are neutral, as is the word 'body' (*soma*): neither 'flesh' nor 'spirit', but capable of being either. In themselves they are certainly not grounds for revulsion, for shame, for anything like guilt; nor are they the 'regrettable appendages' to the soul of Platonism. To Westerners, with a certain inheritance of guilt about bodily and sexual functions, at least if they are sincerely trying to please God in their lives, one is strongly inclined to say:

'God made you as you are, with powerful physical and emotional forces. They are not "sinful" or the result of sin! Rejoice in these forces, and live them. The real enemy that cuts you off from God is guilt or shame about being the creature of God which you are.'

Perhaps this lesson needs emphasizing, especially for men as opposed to women. God provided us all with a digestive and a reproductive system – both essential to the survival and development of the human race – and there can surely be no reason to suppose that God is more interested in the functioning of the reproductive than of the digestive system. As long as we do not harm ourselves (hard to imagine that we can do so seriously with either function) or other people.

Paul's understanding of the risen Lord (as one whom, in order to bring out the meaning of the words *for him*, we are somewhat clumsily calling spirit-body-self) is essential for our grasp of his teaching on the Eucharist.

The controversy in the West about 'real presence' has been bedevilled before, during and after the Reformation by both sides failing to distinguish the state of the mortal Jesus from his state as risen Lord. Jesus' own words, 'This is my body . . . this is the cup of my blood', are not a *distinction* (how could they be, since the blood is part of the body?), but a typically Hebraic *parallelism*: 'This is my body-self [given or broken] for you . . . this is my life poured out for you.' It is clear that we are not, in Paul's thought, concerned with 'the mortal Jesus': 'We celebrate the death of the Lord [the risen One] until he comes' (1 Cor 11:26). We receive the spirit-body-self of the risen Lord to nourish the spirit-life already inaugurated or 'born from above' in us, and to transform us into the spirit-body of Christ – which we already are, though not yet fully.

It is interesting to note that, before the Western mind had set about its ruthless distinctions (which eventually led to such success in the natural sciences), classical Christian literature made no separations between what we might call the three modes in which the Body of Christ exists: the risen Lord, the Church, the Eucharist. They were thought of as one 'mystical' or spiritual reality. Indeed, the term 'mystical body' was first and for long applied to the Eucharistic elements, that is, the Body of Christ in the

Christian mysteries (as H. de Lubac showed some fifty years ago[4]). Only later and by degrees did the Church come to be called 'the mystical Body'. Augustine surprises us in his instructions to neophytes at the Easter Vigil when he explains to them that, when the priest stands before you at Communion with the host and says, 'The Body of Christ', you reply, 'Amen' – meaning, 'Yes, we are.' Only those who *are* the Body of Christ may be nourished by the Body of Christ. So, too, a century earlier, Cyprian wrote: 'When Christ calls bread his body, he was indicating us as a united people he was carrying in his hands.'[5]

Paul carries his Eucharistic 'realism' very far. When condemning the practice of some who came to the Christian assembly, not to share the Lord's supper, but to eat their own meal, and even to drink too much, he warns:

> For anyone who eats and drinks without recognizing the body [of Christ], eats and drinks judgment upon himself. That is why many of you are weak and ill and some of you have died (1 Cor 11:29–30).

However odd we may find the thought, it is quite clear that Paul means by 'judgment' not just something that happens in the mind of God; it consists in the offenders getting ill and dying. Otherwise all would remain alive 'until he comes'. This very realist and bodily understanding of the power of the Eucharist became in later Christian writing the theme of Holy Communion as the 'medicine of immortality, the antidote to death, so that we may ever live in Jesus Christ'.[6]

From the beginning of Christian teaching the Eucharist was seen as a powerful force to enhance the unity of the Body of Christ. We are already one Body because we are baptized into one Body. The gift of unity is God's from the outset. But our Christian unity is not perfect: indeed, one of Paul's chief reasons for writing to his Corinthian converts was the existence of factions there. And we may reflect that we can never be perfectly united with each other until each and all are perfectly united in Christ with the Father.

However, the fact that there is a God-given unity or communion among all who are baptized into Christ, and the fact that unity has always been understood as the chief fruit or effect of the Eucharist, provides a very strong argument for the discreet use of Eucharistic sharing as a means to bring about today the fuller unity of Christians.

The question of Eucharistic sharing or intercommunion is riddled with complexities and anomalies. For instance: Eucharistic sharing between individuals (a married couple) or groups (ecumenical) is not the same as authorized Eucharistic sharing as an approved relationship between (all members of) two Churches who are not in full communion with each other, nor simply divided, but in partial communion. Another anomaly arises from the experience of anyone who, at any level, gets involved in ecumenical activity with other Christians: one at once feels so much more 'in communion with' and recognizes a profound rapport about what 'really matters' in Christian commitment, with *these* members of other Churches than one does with those members of one's own Church. There are, for instance, fundamentalists in any Church ('biblical' in reformed tradition, 'Tridentine' in the Catholic tradition); there are reasonably conservative thinkers – people who stick to the traditional Christian beliefs – who find themselves in something like a love-hate relationship of unity with traditional opponents, over against 'liberal' Christians in various Churches for whom, if it is not fair to say that anything goes, then at least there is a ready tendency to solve some of the paradoxes of Christian belief by denying one half of the paradox in order to keep up with modern opinion. For example, let Jesus be 'just a man', or let Christ be just one among many Christs whom God has raised up in religious history. One could put it acidly from a viewpoint in central London: if All Saints, Margaret Street, and All Souls, Langham Place, are in communion with each other – and they certainly are – what does 'being in communion with' really mean?

Spirituality

It is an obvious step for us to now move on from Pauline body-theology to consider the question of spirituality. Today, the quest for spirituality is fashionable, and it raises some questions and sells like hot cakes – to a perhaps mainly middle-class Christian élite. May one perhaps ponder and probe the following areas:

—'Spirituality' does seems to be something for middle-class Christians. It has not notably drawn the aristocracy into eight-day (or longer) retreats. It has not succeeded in becoming a popular movement. The 'people' cannot afford time or money for retreat houses. And attempts at spreading DIY retreats among 'ordinary' people still seem to reach only the teachers, the professional classes, the retired, and not the 'working' class. And not the young.

—A survey would surely indicate that well-known male spiritual guides attract a predominantly female clientèle; that this is the prevailing pattern (and always has been), whatever other minority situations become common; that the few female guides attract a predominantly male clientèle. This is surely quite proper, but does it gloss the word 'spiritual'?

—May there not be a faint whiff of 'chosen soul' about all this? That is, even when the main drive is an honest attempt to make personal prayer (communication with God) something which is recognized as: (a) available to all; (b) not just a matter of 'saying prayers' according to an approved pattern (approved by others); (c) but an opportunity for all of personal growth.

There is a deep ambiguity in the whole idea of 'spiritual-ity', as previous reflections on body-theology in Paul and other New Testament writers may well suggest. Clearly, there are different *styles* of Christian living, all equally valid, but suited to different clusters of human characteris-tics. There are different 'spiritualities' from the solitary (Carthusian and eremitical), to the enclosed community (Cistercian and Carmelite), to the monastic (Benedictine), itinerant (Franciscan, Dominican) to the outgoing, apos-tolic, missionary, religious order instanced by Mary Ward and Ignatius Loyola; to the modern secular institutes, which seem to have been established to enable people to live religious life in secular situations and without the restrictions of the canon law that applied to religious con-gregations.

And there are honest to God laity variously committed to serving Christ's people. Ignatian spirituality has proved to be among the most flexible, designed as it is to serve any and every form of apostolic commitment, with the demands of mediating Christ's continuing service to peo-ple in need overriding any and every preconceived 'pat-tern' of Christian living. The ideal is flexibility, particularly well captured by the French word *disponibilité*, which makes clear that it is the Lord who calls the tune.

Now that is all very well. But something else has dogged Christian life-styles since the post-apostolic age. Plato, who has never been bettered on the subject of individual ethics, has been the greatest threat to the Gospel throughout the centuries in both East and West. To Plato and his followers the true 'I' is the soul, with the body a regrettable appendage: indeed, worse than regrettable in that it weighs down, corrupts, soils the spirit which naturally tends to fly upwards and fuse with the One, the Absolute. Peter Brown, in his monumentally-learned book, *The Body and Society: Men, Women and Sexual Renunciation in Early Christianity*[1] has traced the all-pervasive influence of Platonism – the only language and idiom of the early cen-turies.

Even though it was the air which all breathed in the Late

Empire, it is very hard to understand how Christianity, born from a Judaism which knew none of it, took on board a doctrine so clean contrary to the Christian Gospel as the natural immortality of the soul; an élitist doctrine; a dualist doctrine; a doctrine despising the work of the Creator who formed man and woman (and not just the human 'soul') in his own image; a doctrine which assumed the superiority of man over woman, of knowledge over love, and regarded the needs of women as a seduction and a snare for men. It is an extraordinary history, since the core of the Christian Gospel is, first, that God saves and imparts his own life to the whole woman and man, no element or part of whom can be thought of as surviving death except by sharing in the Spirit-life of the risen Jesus and thus becoming – not immortal spirit – but Spirit-filled human. Orthodox Christianity (or the Great Church) resisted the many sects which advocated sexual abstinence as the 'true' Christain ideal for all, but even the moderate sexual control advocated by such as Clement of Alexandria was later overcome by more 'platonic' positions, suspicious and scornful of sexual activity. The history of sexual renunciation is the history of those who gave up, as far as they could and with great twistings and turnings, what they regarded as demeaning and degrading and shameful, instead of giving an area of experience to God precisely because it was precious and beautiful and valued. No one spoke up for the positive value of the body and of physical love, as touching on the fullness of humanity promised in eternal life. No one really spoke up for the human, as precisely what God had created, the vehicle of his own love and commitment and self-gift, the reality he wished more and more to fill with his presence.

How accurate, then, is the term 'spirituality' to denote the development of forms of personal prayer, as opposed to public or liturgical prayer? The forms of what might be called 'specialization' in this area in Western Christianity were at the outset somewhat cerebral, or at any rate refined and individualistic. This was clearly part of the general rage for individualism which was characteristic of the

Renaissance in many areas (including moral philosophy or Christian ethics), such as Eucharistic devotion: the individualism was perhaps toned down by a sometimes intense relationship to a director of the other sex. But the 'methods of prayer' concentrated on moving from the conceptual and meditative to imaginative contemplation, and then to persistence in attitudes of 'soul' or 'spirit', or an inward awareness in the centre of the soul. Nothing much bodily arose about this: inward feelings (of the inner or spiritual senses) could be cultivated, but not much in the way of ordinary sensuous feelings. Contemplation was the aim.

An exception was Ignatius Loyola, an incurable romantic, who could never become a Renaissance man but remains irrepressibly vivid. His floods of tears (a daily occurrence), and his 'application' of the senses, could never be quite assimilated by post-mediaeval Western men, who wrote the books, even if they could very easily by women. This surely indicates that the development of personal prayer had been led almost exclusively by men (barring the unassimilable and perhaps neurotic Teresa of Avila) – by men concentrating on the inner and upper.

In quite recent times, however, there has been a strong swing in the direction of the body. Or perhaps it would be more accurate to speak of a surge outward from the inner and individualistic recesses of awareness to full bodily humanity – and out from there to other people in their bodiliness.

To go from the extreme of the solitary, upright figure at the *prie-dieu* (the emblem of individualism) to the pentecostal rave-up is to cover the entire spectrum; private to corporate; inner concentrated awareness to extraversion, with pretty well every bodily manifestation, and with sounds and colourful sights thrown in. One hardly needs to instruct Pentecostalists in methods of prayer.

However, without going all the way to the rave-up, one can pick out various elements which can prove very expressive and helpful in more personal prayer.

Dancing is perhaps the oldest form of religious expression, almost by definition corporate or public, rather than private. It precedes word-prayer as a total human expressive form. It needs no words to interpret or articulate it. Forms of prayer that the East never lost have returned to the West. One can integrate oneself to be in touch with the creating God simply by *feeling* one's multitudinous bodily sensations in a deliberate and developed sensitive awareness.[2] There is no reflection on this feeling, or interpreting of it. It *is* prayer, it *is* communion with the Creator.

Similarly with hearing: being aware of all the sounds of God's creation in a way that puts my inner self in immediate touch with the outer reality of nature and mankind. Not so easy as it sounds. You are not to 'listen to' the sounds, as that can be possessive (taking possession) and interpretative; you just hear and let things and people be. You are 'out there' not 'in here'.

Then there is the more studied hearing involved in listening to music (or playing music). It is an essentially receptive form of prayer, as are all the post-beginner forms, and not a form that depends on my effort.

And any or all of these forms have in recent years been increasingly shared by a group rather than practised in splendid (or strained and painful) isolation. Community, the support of others, has been the discovery. The prayer of the group is found to be more than the sum of its parts (that is, of the individual experiences). Corporate experience can be extremely powerful – for good or for ill.

All this activity ties in with the revived interest in Celtic spirituality, which involves a deeply sensitive rapport with living nature – a sense of its unity, its aspiring to God together, sometimes its 'groaning in travail together' (Rom 8:22).[3]

And surely the very positive treatment of sexual attachment and sexual activity is one of the major fruits and blessings of this return to wholeness, or return to the Bible, if you wish. Who has expressed it with more delicate conviction and thoroughness than Rosemary Haughton? In her at once exuberant and controlled exploration of passion, *The Passionate God*, she writes of truthfulness and untruthful deception in touching with our hands:

But the same thing applies to specifically sexual parts and actions. It is more difficult to understand wisely in this area because the emotions involved are so profound and so violent, but the same kind of insight is needed. The symbolism of the actions of human sexual intercourse is inherent, and this applies to those parts which are not seen, the places where the seed grows in the man and is implanted in the woman. But the fact that the bodies of men and women have different functions and forms adds a dimension which was absent in considering hands. The need of one for the other in order that the act of generation may be completed is an essential element in the meaning of the body as sexual. On the very precise interaction of two bodies depends the degree of pleasure which they are able to share, and this giving and taking is of whole persons, a giving and taking which draws to a point of exchange all the levels of sharedness which make up human life, from the most earthy to the most heavenly. And it becomes heavenly not by distancing itself from the physical and 'offering' all this to God, but precisely by paying detailed and loving attention to what is being done, and precisely how.'[4]

This is a very far cry from the purpose of the body as set forth by Origen.

Do not think that just as 'the belly' is made 'for food and food for the belly', that in the same way the body is made for intercourse. If you wish to understand the Apostle's train of reasoning, for what reason the body was made, then listen: it was made that it should be a 'temple to the Lord'; that the soul, being holy and blessed, should act in it as if it were a priest serving before the Holy Spirit that dwells in you. In this manner, Adam had a body in Paradise; but in Paradise he did not 'know' Eve.[5]

Negatively: the strained, sustained effort to be spiritual and to persevere in *seeking* God through the privation of human needs, can kill the life and meaning of living faith, particularly in sensitive, artistic people. Whereas the red-blooded finding of God in all the realities of living touches on the Absolute. Why did so many centuries of Christian effort think they could improve on the way God had made men and women. Women? Some few were caught up in the continuing struggle to be ethereal, almost always dedicated to the Church as children by their parents to be 'sacred virgins' – and so not a financial liability on the family. But the great majority were discarded, suspected, treated as mere seducers and sources of temptation. Only in our day are we positively encouraged to touch on the ecstatic and the eternal, to be in touch with our own and the other's deepest and fullest self through sexual activity.

So maybe 'spirituality' is no longer the best description for confident contact with God through the realities of human, bodily living.

Sharing Communion

The title of this chapter comes from the book *Sharing Communion*, edited by Melanie Finch and Ruth Reardon, and to which I contributed some 'Conclusions' when it was published in 1983.[1]

The book arose from a survey conducted among married couples who comprised a practising Roman Catholic and an equally committed member of another Christian Church (in England). The couples state their thoughts, attitudes, practices in the matter of sharing Holy Communion.

Theology from Experience

It hardly seems necessary to spell out the personal distress, even anguish, suffered by so many couples when they find themselves unable to share Eucharistic communion together.

What we have to ask ourselves is whether we are listening to a Christian theology of a different kind, and from a different source, than that which normally circulates in the Churches – a theology with at least as much right to be heard and to shape our decisions as any other. The point is that these people care, and care deeply, not only about Christ, the Church, the Eucharist, but about Christian unity. They are not some maverick group of loosely attached Christians, or some passing fashion. They are the sort of people who are central to any Church. And they are not going to go away. Theirs is a theology arising from lived and deeply committed Christian experience. And what other source has theology but personal, committed, lived Christian faith? Their forms of expression, charged as they are with feeling, may occasionally jar. But they challenge strongly the cooler forms of theological judgment which descend on them, as it were, from above in classical formulas, outlining classical positions. Theirs, too, is the voice of people who know about, and care about, the Christian family, the domestic brick out of which all our Churches are built.

The position of the *sensus fidelium* as a source of Christian truth is ambiguous in Catholic theology. An older theology with a mainly down-from-above view regarded the body of believing Christians simply as 'the learning Church' at the receiving end from 'the teaching Church'. But re-emphasis on the gifts that the Spirit of God gives to all Christians has revived the view that 'the people of God' are a source of insight separate from, a source of authority different from, that belonging either to learning or to pastoral office. It is not that one can reach Christian truth by Gallup polls or by counting heads. It is, rather, that the voice of the Spirit may be discerned, and heard differently, among those whose lives show a special commitment to Christ in his Church. He does not hand over his prophetic ministry to one part of his Body to be exercised in his place, but continues to exercise it himself in all.

Developing Unity

Looking at the couples in the survey, a certain progression is observable within each group and from group to group. Older couples started their marriage when relations between the Churches were frostier, and with a considerable sense of isolation. Younger couples have inherited the ecumenical thaw, and find more understanding of and sympathy with their situation from their pastors, and the opportunity of support and the fruit of experience from other couples. They regard it from the outset as much more normal to learn about and to share in the traditions of worship and spirituality of their two Churches. And this is a cumulative and developing experience which presses forward towards the fullest possible unity.

The progression within each group is markedly affected by the arrival of children and by the parents' approach to communicant age. Parents begin apart, nurtured in two different Churches, each finding the other somewhat strange, and no doubt with a certain cargo of tribal prejudices they have taken on board. It is the differences which loom large. They learn to develop their own personal Christian unity within their marriage, and in the course of this process the differences move to the margin and the deep realities of their common inheritance become central. It is the unity which Christ gives, the unity which all our divisions can never destroy and which they have discovered as a reality for themselves, which they pass on to their children. For the children, this unity that is deeper than the diversities is there from the beginning. If there is no strain between the parents, none is passed on to the children. For them a unity deeper than diversity is normal – it is not a problem; they have no other experience. It then becomes more and more pressing for the parents that the family should remain united in their dual allegiance and should share their Christian life fully together. Left to themselves, adults can assimiliate and live tensions, gauge external pressures (such as what others might think, and whether a course of action may produce more divisions than unity), and tailor their actions accordingly. Children cannot. Hence the children's needs become the needs of the family as a family, and increasingly modify the attitudes and practices of the parents. This is the cross on which the parents are pinned: the values and emphases of the Churches to which they are devoted; the needs of the united Christian family. The Churches tend to regard them as marginal; it is understandable if they come to regard the Churches as marginal in their family, particularly as they are living the Christian unity about which the Churches discourse.

Global and Domestic Church

The present discipline of their Church in Britain leads a number of Roman Catholics to worship more frequently in their partner's Church than in their own, and to find there the fulfilment of precisely those spiritual needs which arise in an inter-Church family. For them this only comes about gradually, and with sadness and reluctance. For their pastors it clearly presents something of a dilemma.

On the one hand there are principles to be maintained which are close to the heart of Roman Catholic thinking, feeling, self-understanding. On the other hand, Roman Catholic discipline comes over as insensitive, unwelcoming, unloving, to a point where committed Roman Catholics themselves are unable to recognize in it a mediation of the person of Christ, or the voice of his Spirit who is always a force of union and reconciliation.

Hence the survey confronts the pastors of the Roman Catholic Church with a certain amount of indiscipline which is too unhappy to be defiant. Such a situation can be variously judged. But one thing is clear: Roman Catholic spouses in inter-Church marriages who receive communion in their spouse's Church usually do so only after much heart-searching, and in the eventual conviction that, in discerning the mind of Christ in the unwelcome situation of division, they must put their marriage, precisely as a Christian marriage, first.

The Roman Catholic emphasis is on the close relation between ecclesial communion (local or regional Churches being in full communion with each other) and Eucharistic communion.

The Church is essentially Eucharistic communion. And so the rules are drawn for whole bodies of Christians which are separated from each other, and who to that extent deny the vision of the *ecclesia catholica* for which the Roman Catholic Church stands: let them first unite, and then share the Eucharist together.

But does that theology fully make sense when applied to a Christian family? Are the members of that family not in full communion with each other?

The Church is a mystery as *Lumen Gentium* proclaims. So no single theology of the Church, however profound and essential its insights, will exhaust its reality. The global and the domestic theologies of the Church are both valid, and pastoral practice needs to accommodate both.

The Eucharist as a Means to Unity

The couples in the survey found that, with very few exceptions, Roman Catholic bishops do not think they have the authority to admit the non-Catholic partner in inter-Church marriage to communion or do not think that the responsibility of decision rests with them. There is something of a stalemate or vicious circle here. This situation has been changed by the *Directory for the Application of Principles and Norms on Ecumenism* issued by the Vatican in March 1993, which clearly states that bishops may admit non-Catholic spouses to Holy Communion on special occasions.

The Roman Catholic documentation on admission to Eucharistic communion of members of other Churches shows two trends.

Commendation of Eucharistic Sharing

The first trend is of an apparent closing by the Secretariat for Promoting Christian Unity of doors opened by Vatican II. The *Decree on Ecumenism* says:

> As for common worship, however, it may not be regarded as a means to be used indiscriminately for the restoration of unity among Christians. Such worship depends chiefly upon two principles: it should signify the unity of the Church; it should provide a sharing in the means of grace. The fact that it should signify unity generally rules out common worship. Yet the gaining of a needed grace sometimes commends it.
>
> The practical course to be adopted, after due regard has been given to all the circumstances of time, place and persons, is left to the prudent decision of the local episcopal authority, unless the Bishops' Conference, according to its own statutes, or the Holy See, has determined otherwise.[2]

The term 'common worship' translates *communicatio in sacris* and certainly includes the Eucharist, as can be seen from the application of the principles to Eastern Christians. The Council manifestly did not hold the principle that Eucharistic communion is solely the end and may never be used as a means for establishing unity. What may not be used *indiscriminately* for the restoration of unity may be used with discrimination. If the fact that common worship should signify unity *generally* (*communiter*) rules it out, then it does not always do so. The *Decree on the Eastern Catholic Churches*,[3] both in theory and in practical rulings, expressly sanctions admission to communion as a means to bring about unity. Eastern Christians, even those from churches which do not accept the 'orthodox' doctrine of the Trinity and Incarnation, are to be admitted to the Eucharist

> . . . if they ask of their own accord and have the right dispositions' – no other conditions are laid down; this is permitted 'in order to promote closer union.'[4]

For Western Christians, however, the Secretariat seemed to be trying to close the door. The *Ecumenical Directory*[5] instanced such extreme cases ('during persecution, in prisons') that it seemed to be saying, 'for practical purposes, never'; but it went on to say that 'in other cases the judge of this urgent necessity must be the diocesan bishop or the Episcopal Conference'.[6]

The *Instruction*[7] of 1972 and the *Interpretative Note*[8] of 1973 softened matters somewhat: the emphasis switched from dramatic physical circumstances to spiritual need, and 'urgent necessity' was changed to 'serious spiritual need'. Hence discretion and authority *does* lie with the bishops in such cases. However, while insisting that *Directory* and *Instruction* 'in no way intended to change the norms set down by the Council's Decree on Ecumenism', the *Interpretative Note* (which has only the authority of its signatories) appeared formally to contradict the Council's teaching by asserting that Eucharistic sharing by those not in full communion 'cannot be considered as an appropriate means for bringing about the fullness of communion'. A benign interpretation would be that general admission to communion all round would not bring about unity: and everyone would agree with that. But it is understandable if bishops are somewhat confused, and have seized on the quite unfounded idea that it is the official Catholic position that admission to Eucharistic communion is never allowed as a means to promote unity.

Individualist and Corporate Aspects

The second main trend in Roman documentation on admission is that, whereas the *Constitution on the Liturgy*[9] recaptured the theology of the Eucharist as essentially a communal celebration, and freed the Roman Catholic Church from the excessively individualistic understanding of Holy Communion which had so long prevailed, the *Decree on Ecumenism* and the subsequent documents depending on it are still thinking solely in terms of the spiritual need of the individual. It is in that context that one of the conditions for admission to communion must be understood, that the non-Catholic be separated from the ministry of his or her own Church. There is no reflection on the needs of ecumenical communities, of which the two-Church family is the prime example. Their need is that of a family as a family: domestic Church. As there is no specific advertence in official documents to their spiritual needs, it rests solely and wholly with their bishops to care for them, bearing in mind their Church's principle that Eucharistic sharing *may* be used with discrimination as a means to promote unity.

The couples do not see the admission of the non-Catholic partner to communion as likely to hinder progress towards unity. They are not a large number, and to meet their spiritual need would open no floodgate. They are, rather, a small qualitative force for unity, already living a measure of unity well beyond that which their Churches enjoy, and needing to be nourished. They are united in baptism; they are united in marriage; they are united in responsibility for the Christian upbringing of their children; their aim for themselves and for others is unity. They think they would be *more* a force for unity rather than less, if they were able to receive communion together openly and with the full blessing of both their Churches.

And is this not an area where those who have some experience of Eucharistic sharing are entitled to judge? With all the ecumenical advances that have been made in recent years, there are still extremely few members of any Church, ordained or lay, who really, concretely and sincerely, even desire to share the Eucharist with other Christians. It should at least be a matter of rejoicing that these couples, these families, do most insistently need and ask to do so.

13

Transformation

When Paul was writing 1 Corinthians, as we have seen, he was inclined to think that some Christians had become ill and died before Christ's coming, because of their misuse of the Eucharist. By the time of the Second Letter to Corinth (probably Paul's fourth at least), he seems to have had second thoughts, both because of the passage of time and because of the perils he had been through himself (2 Cor 11:23–33). He had come to realize that he, too, might die before Christ's coming. Further, it is clear that his answers on the matter of our resurrection had not settled anxieties and disputes, so he returns to the question of our transformation from baptism onwards into the Spirit-self of the risen Lord.

In the very elliptical passage in 2 Cor 5:1–10, Paul tries to explain further in terms of the very striking, but in many ways awkward, picture of the risen Christ being himself a 'tent-house', which or whom we progressively put on.

The reason for his choosing this image, evoking the Jerusalem temple, seems to be that it takes up Jesus' saying about his own life, brought in evidence against him (Mk 14:57–8) at his trial:

> And some stood up and bore false witness against him, saying, 'We heard him say, "I will destroy this temple that is made with hands, and in three days I will build another not made with hands". '.

Mark says it was false witness. John records another version of what Jesus said at the cleansing of the temple. In Jn 2:19–22:

> Jesus said: 'Destroy this temple and in three days I will raise it up.' But he spoke of the temple of his body. When therefore he was raised from the dead, his disciples remembered that he had said this, and they believed the scripture and the saying of Jesus.

The scripture referred to is Psalm 69:9. ('The zeal of thy house has consumed me.') This adumbrates Jesus' zeal for cleansing the temple, and was quoted by John (Jn 2:17). Christian witness from the outset saw the risen Jesus as the true temple in whom God's glory dwelt (so, Jn 1:14), and themselves as that temple insofar as he dwelt in them, and they in him.

Paul's picture in 2 Cor is best understood within the idea of a pilgrimage through the desert of this life from baptism to the fullness of God's kingdom, like the journey of the Jews from Egypt into the Promised Land. So, with these images in mind we may paraphrase 2 Cor 5:1–10, as follows.

1 It is common Christian belief that (as Jesus promised), if our earthly temple be destroyed, we already have from God a temple (Christ) not made with human hands (as was the Jerusalem temple), but an eternal and heavenly dwelling.
2 And what is more, in our present situation we groan inwardly, eagerly longing to put on this further heavenly dwelling.
3 So long as, when we have put it on, we do not turn out to be morally naked.
4 Indeed, in our present body-dwelling we groan and are weighed down, in that we do not just want to be stripped (of mortality), but to put the further dwelling on, so that what is mortal in us may be swallowed up by life.
5 But it is God himself who has worked upon us for this

very end, in having given us the first instalment of the Spirit.

6 So, being always in good heart, and realizing that while we are 'at home' in our mortal body, we are 'away' from the Lord.

7 For we voyage by faith and not by sight.

8 We are in good heart and would wish rather to be 'away' from our mortal body and 'at home' with the Lord.

9 Hence, whether 'at home' or 'away', we are all the while anxious about pleasing him.

10 For we must all be exposed before the judgment seat of Christ, so that each may receive good or evil for what he did through the body.

There are many echoes of this belief and imagery in other Pauline writings (Rom 8:17–30 especially) where Paul is similarly concerned with the holy living of Christians – not by the forces and standards of the 'flesh', but by those of the Spirit. Insofar as Christ is in us now by his Spirit, to that extent we are alive by his life, and God will surely raise us up as he raised Jesus (Rom 8:9–11). Indeed, Paul sees the whole of creation 'groaning in travail' in the grip of demonic powers of destruction, and 'waiting with eager longing' to be set free along with us; we too, who already have from baptism the first instalment of the Spirit, 'groan inwardly as we wait for adoptions as sons, the redemption of our bodies' (Rom 8:23).

Paul had already written (1 Cor 15:53–4) of the necessity for 'the mortal' of our present bodily state to 'put on' immortality, so that 'death should be swallowed up by victory' (Is 25:8). The passage from 2 Cor, however, comes within a wider context of transformation theology, which has already been the theme of 2 Cor 3:7 to 4:18. To understand the force of Paul's imagery here, we need first to recall the understanding of vision among the ancients. They thought the eye was an aperture through which light entered the head, so that, with the head filled with light, one could see.

Thus, Jesus can say (Mt 6:22–3):

The eye is the lamp of the body. If your eye is clear and unimpeded, your whole body will be full of light; but if your eye is obstructed, your whole body will be full of darkness [that is, you won't be able to see].

So, if what should be light to you is darkness, then how blind will you be?

In 2 Cor 3:1–6, Paul briefly reviews his contrast between Law and Spirit and his argument (elaborated elsewhere) that the Old Covenant, made known as written Law or code, led to death and was to be superseded; whereas the New Covenant, inscribed by the Spirit in the human heart, as Jeremiah had promised (Jer 31:31), leads to unlimited life. Then he picks up the story of Moses coming down from the mountain with the tablets of the Law (2 Cor 3:7), as it is given in Exodus (Ex 34:29–35).

The face of Moses shone with dazzling brightness, because he had been looking open-eyed on the bright glory of God himself: that light had entered his head and made his own countenance blaze.

Paul then, in a passage that can only be fully understood in terms of Jewish Christians who despised Paul's 'lowly' authority in favour of the teaching of some showy ecstatics at Corinth, sets aside this merely external dazzle of the exceptional leader (Moses), which was due to fade anyway, because the Old Covenant is abrogated by the New; and points in its place to the far greater glory which can be shared and hoped for by *all* Christians. In language drawn from the story of the transfiguration Paul says that, by open-eyed contemplation of the glory of God as it is mirrored in Christ, we are interiorly transformed into him who is the very image of God (2 Cor 3:18). The splendour that shines out from Christ does not merely enlighten the eyes of our minds (though it does do that): it changes us in our depths into him. The light that enters us is a creative and transforming power.

The same thinking seems to underlie a quite different writer, who promises: 'We shall be like him because we shall see him as he is' (1 Jn 3:2): seeing him as he is, and being filled with the full force of his light, makes us like him. In 2 Cor 4:6, Paul returns to the same image by referring to Is 9:2: 'The people who were walking in the darkness see a great light; on us, dwellers in the land of shadow and death, a great light will shine.'

The true preachers of the gospel are not chosen ecstatics, special souls, giving merely external manifestations of 'inspiration' (as some at Corinth hold); they are simply servants, slaves ministering in weakness. On them, as they sit in darkness, God has made a great light to shine, in that they are illumined interiorly in their hearts and minds by the glory that shines in the face of Jesus Christ.

In very similar circumstances to those in which he wrote to Corinth, Paul writes from prison to his beloved converts at Philippi – a Roman *colonia* whose members all shared in the privileges and rights of Roman citizenship:

> *Our* citizenship is in heaven, and it is from there that we eagerly await a Saviour, Jesus Christ the Lord. He will transform our miserable body [body self], conforming it to his glorious body in virtue of the power and dominion that he exercises over all things (Phil 3:20–1).

There has, then, first to be the eager longing, the vast emptiness – and then the risen Lord takes possession.

We may well feel our hearts warmed by this doctrine of interior transformation and shared 'glory', and yet wonder what it has to do with real life as we experience it in the daily round; but the thrust and hallmark of Paul's vision, belief, teaching, are that it is precisely in and through the ordinariness of life, its rough and tumble, that the interior transformation into the likeness of Christ, the very image of God's glory, takes place. Repeatedly he sets himself against 'special souls' and unusual manifestations and comes back to the hardships, rejections, suffering, indeed the sheer slog, of life as the process of being shaped into the image of Jesus, who became the Christ and the Lord precisely and only through death and the cross. And one has seen it repeatedly in life – the depth of spirituality that grows in endurance, in selflessness, sometimes in acute loss and suffering; the shallowness of self-satisfaction and easy success giving place to a true expansion of spirit, as the unsatisfied longing of the human heart grows. There has to be space, emptiness, before God can fill it. Certainly, Paul's message is that it is in the texture of real life that the light of Christ can enter into and transform the flesh-self into Spirit-self.

As already noted, Paul's language of transformation is that used in the story of Jesus' transfiguration in the synoptic gospels. Sometimes modern commentators consider this to be the story of an appearance to his followers of the risen Christ, which has been put back into Jesus' public life. Be that as it may, the point of the story where it now stands in the gospels is that Peter, James and John are given a vision of the true reality of Jesus, the everyday Jesus they now know.

As writers in the Greek Orthodox tradition often point out, the transfiguration is not a change in Jesus but in the vision of the apostles. They are briefly enabled to see the glory of God in the face and figure of the living Jesus. When the vision fades, they look up and see no one but 'only Jesus'.

And that is Paul's constant lesson too. The growth of 'spirituality' in us, the reshaping of our inner body self by, and after the pattern of, the risen Lord is an ability to see the glory of God in the ordinariness, inadequacies, frustrations, rejections, sufferings of human life. Paul asserts that he had every advantage available under the Old Covenant:

> But all such assets I have written off because of Christ. I would say more: I count everything sheer loss, because all is far outweighed by the gain of knowing Christ Jesus my Lord, for whose sake I did in fact lose everything. I count it so much garbage for the sake of gaining Christ and finding myself incorporate in him, with no righteousness of my own, no legal rectitude, but the righteousness which comes from faith in Christ, given by God in response to faith. All I care for is to know Christ, to experience the power of his resur-

rection, and to share his sufferings, in growing conformity with his death, if only I may finally arrive at the resurrection from the dead (Phil 3:7–11).

14

Paul on Sin

St Paul's teaching on sin is found in its complete form in Rom 5–7, with some amplification in Rom 8. The key to understanding Paul's unfamiliar imagery and very complicated sentences – made harder by his breaking off in the middle of a sentence in Rom 5:12 and starting it again in Rom 5:18 – is to be found in a right understanding of Rom 5:12. It has usually been assumed that Paul *must* want to say that sin caused death, and so the verse has been translated:

> Therefore, as sin came into the world through one man and death through sin, and so death spread to all men *because* all men sinned.[1]

However, startling though it may at first seem, he says the converse, namely:

> Therefore, as sin came into the world through one man and death through sin, and so death spread to all men, *whereupon* all sinned.[2]

The use of the Greek preposition *epi* with the dative to express succession of events is well attested.

The clue to this otherwise puzzling logic is that Paul shares much of the mythical thought of his time. He envisages both sin and death as demonic forces – or a single demonic power – that attach to and destroy men and women: a single power of corruption that weakens and finally destroys us, both morally (sin) and physically (death). So his understanding is that Adam, by his disobeying of God's command not to eat the fruit, let 'death' loose in the world, and himself died. So, one sin let in death which then attacks all as a corrosive force, whereupon all sin. So man is enslaved to the destroying power of sin and death. God, Paul explains, gave the Law to show man the paths of right living and so clear his moral blindness – but the Law does not give us the power to do what is seen to be right; so it only had the result of putting Israel in bad faith by comparison with the uninstructed gentiles: like Adam, they now disobey explicit precepts of God, so their sin is worse (a hard doctrine).

Paul then develops a point-by-point contrast between the one man Adam and the new man Christ: Christ exactly counterbalances and counteracts the damage done by Adam. Indeed, he goes further and gives man more than the paradisal life he had lost.

By his *obedience* (*cf* Phil 2:8) Christ conquers the demonic powers that enslave man; even man's last enemy, death, is vanquished by Christ's resurrection (1 Cor 15:25–6). The risen Lord then sends his Spirit, from the Father (Rom 6:12–14, amplified in Rom 8:9–11): the Spirit gives to man precisely the *power* (for he is the life force of God) to avoid evil and conquer death. So, by faith in Jesus Christ we receive the power to do good and overcome death: we share in the life force of God.

We are freed by the Spirit, not only from sin and resulting death, but from Law. We are freed from Law as a dispensation governing our relationship with God, which is no longer that of commandment and obedience, but the personal relationship of sonship: love. So we are freed from Law-as-code, and cannot please God by obeying rules – but we are not freed from Law as compulsion, for the love of God is the driving force of human life (as Augustine so well understood), whether we know it or not. Indeed, Paul goes on to speak of the new 'slavery' that the freedom of the children of God involves: we, 'who were slaves of sin leading to death, have become slaves of righteousness leading to life' (Rom 6:15–18).

In 1 Cor 15:55–7, Paul makes use of the same mythical imagery, with a slight modification: 'death' is seen as a scorpion, planting the sting of sin in man ('the sting of death is sin'); and the sting is powered by the Law ('the power of sin is the Law'), which makes wrongdoing into disobedience; but Christ conquers the agent, the scorpion itself death, so that it can no longer implant the sting of sin.

We may at this point stand back from Paul's text to ask what we can possibly make today of these mythical 'demonic forces' on which his understanding rests. We are unlikely to be able to regard them as very devilish beings, horned tail and all: but did Paul?

The mythological image represents for him and for us, as no other could, the profound mysteries of our human life and experience. We cannot comprehend, as we could understand a man-made mechanism subject to our control, how the death and resurrection of Christ not only save us from Law-sin-death, but even give us a share in God's life. This awareness of life everlasting is a dimension of our present human experience: not only in our hatred of suffering, weakness and death, but in our reaching out beyond the highest joys and fullness of life towards life that is perfect and indestructible. So, too, there is something beyond the human in our experience of the injustice of life and the fathomless capacity of man for wickedness (as in drug pushing, torture, concentration camps, gas chambers): there is something that can only be called demonic. Only mythical imagery can convey the truth.

Next, it must be observed that what became of the classical doctrine of original sin is not to be found in Paul. It may be that we inherit the weakness of all our ancestors, both in our psychic make-up and in the world as it surrounds us – though it is also true that we inherit all that is good in both. But Paul does not say so in Rom 5 (or anywhere else). He says that Adam 'let in' the force of corruption, which then attacks us all. The idea that we inherit from Adam an internal flaw is very largely due to Augustine, who was translating the Latin version (*in quo omnes peccaverunt*) of the end of Rom 5:12: he rendered it, not as 'because all sinned', nor as 'whereupon all sinned', but as 'in whom all sinned' (that the Greek could not possibly mean).

In Rom 7 Paul does go on to speak of our experience of moral weakness, and of our inability to do the good we aspire to, in terms that recall the rabbinical doctrine of the *yecer hara*. This has usually been translated 'concupiscence', or the inability of reason to control passion, of which we are all aware; but in rabbinical theology it is something that is implanted in us by God, and should be represented by a neutral word such as 'libido'.

By it is meant the 'go-go' element in human make-up, which accounts for all the creative energy for discovery and initiative in human life, and without which life would slow down and stop. It is the equivalent of Plato's *thumos*. It can produce evil, but can also produce great good. So, in Paul's understanding, and as is indeed obvious from our experience, we are not by faith in Christ immune from attack by 'sin-death': but we are not enslaved – we have the power of the Spirit to resist, and to pick ourselves up and start again.

Next, it should be observed that Paul is not talking about *sins*, but about *sin*. And this is very important. Great saints have been acutely aware of their sin, whereas rumbustious sinners can be blind to it. It is sometimes said that people today have lost a sense of sin – yes, they are often aware of sins, but have lost a sense of sin. Sins can be very trivial, and it is hard to believe that God is much interested in the petty and repetitive laundry list that we regularly take to confession.

Sin is extremely important. It is the distance that lies between our present state and the transformation into the likeness of Christ which God is working in us. It is everything in us that separates us from God and prevents total response to, total commitment to, the Lord. A sense of sin is the product of love for God, and that is why 'the saints' have it strongly.

But it is not altogether our fault, though we can of course add to the distance or disintegration by our conduct, just as we can allow God to heal sin. We are not to blame for 'sin': both because, being finite and created, we cannot be perfect and because, being creatures destined to grow from infancy to full maturity, we cannot be at the end of the road while on the journey. So, no guilt about sin. Certainly, guilt for all sins, which are the result of sin; but not out of proportion or melodramatically.

And, of course, 'sin' is forgiven in advance by the redeeming Spirit of the Lord. Christ has already won that victory. We are freed from Law-sin-death into the freedom of the children of God. Jesus is the Lamb of God who takes away the sin of the world; how tiresome that liturgical texts say 'sins' at this point!

Finally, because we are pilgrims still on the way and still under attack, Paul gives many general guidelines for Christian living, usually in the moral exhortation at the end of his letters. But they are not code Law. They are the 'pedagogue' (child leader) to Christ, the slave who led children to school, with whose services we can never wholly dispense, because we are never wholly mature but always becoming so. In the same way, Jesus, in the Sermon on the Mount and in his other sayings, described many challenges to show wherein true discipleship lies – challenges to the best we can do, the highest of our insights, the most exhaustive of our plans; challenges of the Gospel, which can never be translated without remainder into Law. They are Gospel, not Law. They are good news, telling us of the greatness that God gives. We will not grow into Christ by keeping rules: at best we will stay where we are.

15

Original Sin Revisited

'Original sin' is a bundle of ideas which first of all need distinguishing one from another before there is any chance of seeing how they are interrelated. The chief strands are: all of us need redemption by Christ; the idea of a fall from a state of super perfection; a fall from 'original justice' into a state of sin and alienation; the transmission of moral weakness; the actual components of character, for good or ill, with which we are born; death regarded as resulting from sin; the collective sinfulness of the world into which we are born; comprehensive biblical ideas of all these forces of disintegration; and, finally, the transmission of what might be called sin.

In addition there are wider theological topics impinging on the whole idea of original sin, some of which are too big to treat adequately here, though they cannot be ignored. These are: the right understanding of Genesis; general biblical ideas of sin; the relation of nature to grace; and the question, 'What does baptism do?' Then there is the Immaculate Conception, also the salvation of all mankind, including non-Christians.

I will treat these themes in a disconnected way – and then see if any sort of synthesis emerges. Theology, of course, can be *too* systematic and it is often better as related themes.

Redemption

The need of redemption by Christ is central to the topic,

though some theologians today (for example, Hick[1]) abandon this crucial tenet: for them, Christ is *a* saviour, one among many, simply one manifestation of God's will. The word 'heresy' really means picking and choosing: what could be easier in solving a dilemma than to suppress one half of it? Much of Karl Rahner's work centres on the problem of the salvation of the unbeliever (so called). Hick, however, is scornful of Rahner's solution in terms of 'anonymous Christians', having failed to grasp the point at issue.[2] Historically, man's need of Christ's saving work has been the central tenet of Christianity.

Genesis

Modern biblical scholarship has made clear that there are different traditions underlying Genesis: the tenth century Jahwist; the ninth century Elohist; the eighth century joining of the Jahwist and Elohist; the seventh century Deuteronomist; and the sixth century Priestly – and there was later editing, as well as the use of legal and mythical material common to near-Eastern peoples (for example, Babylonian cosmology).

The fact that Genesis uses current myths *and* includes two creation accounts that are inconsistent with one another shows that Genesis as it stands is not trying to teach the literal truth of its story. The first, the Priestly account (the latest), is in stylized literary form and it is the second, Jahwist, account that is the older and has the story of the Fall.

What Genesis chiefly sets forth are these truths: that God is the sole source and origin of all that is (the word *arche* can mean 'source' as well as 'beginning') and it is anti-dualist by contrast with the Babylonian myths, which are polytheist and dualist; all God's work is good; God's purpose in creating at all is to produce Israel (the genesis of the people); woman's equality with man is demonstrated in that God cut the human reality (Adam) in half (a recent article[3] shows that the Hebrew word chosen for Adam's 'rib' really means 'side') to produce both the male and the female (end of argument about woman being derived from man!); and, finally, the goodness of marriage. 'Adam' means a human being, so Adam is both a typical figure and a particular male in the myth. Today, theologians see the truth of the story to lie in the religious ideas that they show to be developing. The Eden story is very restrained, showing mankind losing confidence before God and demonstrating that, divided from God, man becomes divided within himself (ashamed) and from other men.

The whole book of Genesis, indeed the Pentateuch (the first five books) and Deuteronomic history (*c*650–550) is concerned with the descent of man from ancestors, and it clearly believes in a legacy of religious downfall (historical and moral) and a process whereby the collective sins of ancestors are visited on their children. Within this overall view the Eden story is an aetiological[4] myth (that is, a story going back to the primordial times to explain the present state of affairs, the problem of evil), to show that evil comes not from God but from creatures. God foretells Adam and Eve that their descendants will be involved in the struggle with evil. The Babel story shows the growing division between men (not women!). Adam, being from the dust, is not 'naturally immortal' and the 'death' that results from disobedience must be given a wider and more religious existential sense than mere physical death: corruption, alienation, disintegration. In the cosmological picture Sheol is furthest away from God, out of his mind and concern, non-existence being a far too sophisticated idea for that time. Both death and life now have a forbidding aspect.

One cannot conclude that Genesis teaches any doctrine of an *inherent* flaw or lack of personal relationship to God, passed on to every individual, through the process of generation, as a result of the sin of an original pair. But it does present the picture of a primordial state lost for his descendants by Adam.

Original Justice and Preternatural Gifts

The Council of Trent in its decree on original sin quoted

and gave more solemn form to many phrases from the anti-Pelagian councils that preceded it, namely the Council of Carthage (428) and the Council of Orange (529). Clearly, at Trent the Adam story was taken literally. The decree is not a chapter followed by canons but consists of five lengthy canons and an appendix on Our Lady. It clearly teaches an original state of 'holiness and justness' lost by Adam for all of humanity. This is what may be called the basis for the Fall doctrine and it presupposes Adam in Eden being at a great height of religious and other perfection, and losing this state for himself and for all of us.

This idea can be seen to grow in the Christian writers of the first five centuries. Irenaeus (late second century) sees man as a child, morally, spiritually, intellectually – as primitive – but destined to grow in stature in all these ways, in harmony with God, starting from a simple and familiar relationship with him. This is much more like Genesis than later views. And it is a remarkably modern and evolutionary view of man, enabling one to think of the *possibility* of a growing cleavage or alienation as man grows culturally from a primitive state – and to think in modern terms of heredity too. It *excludes* the idea of a previous or original state of mature perfection and of a fall from that state as a once-for-all event; and the idea of the originating sin as the same reality in all of us.But later writers did not stay with Irenaeus, but allegorized and romanticized Genesis progressively. They also philosophized in platonic terms – for example, man's primitive grasp of the whole realm of ideas. In the process they built up a more enhanced view of man's primitive state, both in terms of mature *religious* perfection and of human perfection. Some of these ideas are to be found in Jewish apocrypha.

Augustine, whose work became the Western tradition, shows the full extent of this development – full control of the passions by reason: integrity as opposed to concupiscence (lack of control of the passions by reason); surpassing intellectual gifts; immunity from physical ills; immortality within his grasp if he continued to feed on the tree of life, which is *not* natural immortality; and, religiously, a state of illumination, beatitude, *posse non peccare*. These ideas of pre-sin Adam affect the picture of Christ that is built up in its turn. The more Adam was built up, the more evil his disobedience was seen to be, and the wider could its repercussions be thought to spread.

The Roman Catholic Church has never made any formal pronouncements on the preternatural gifts. Trent confined itself to the religious aspects: as a result of original sin, man was changed for the worse in body and soul – this mainly to exclude the idea that death and not damage to the soul was the only result of original sin. Man lost his holiness and justness and became liable to concupiscence.

Ideas of 'supernatural' or 'preternatural' are inappropriate to the Bible itself, for nowhere in it is the idea of 'nature' that they presuppose. In the Old Testament 'nature' is man before God (that is, always the perspective of the Bible), nor does it anywhere attribute man's present condition to the one sin of Adam.

Patristic tradition, as we have seen, is varied. Today it may be legitimate to give to the idea of original justness an eschatological sense, but this would mean putting together many ideas not yet developed. Here, then, a mere sketch: man was created in and for Christ; this is his origin rather than a state in which he once was and from which he fell; patristic allegorizing of Genesis points as much to an *idealized* picture of Adam as to a literal belief; there is in man always a force tending towards holiness and justness, that is towards Christ; there is always also a force pulling against and preventing the Christward force having its full effect; so there would be a progressive fall from original justness. Hence, original justness and preternatural gifts are what man was destined to become.

Again, our understanding of the original sin bundle of ideas must be Christological – indeed, there surely cannot be a necessary belief that is *not* about Christ.

Biblical Ideas of Sin

The idea of sin develops progressively in the Bible. In the

older layers of the Old Testament, God's election and initiative come first. Israel is God's people by his choice, not if and insofar as she obeys cultic and moral commands: this is unconditional love. Commandments are added as man's response, but they are few, simple and easy to fulfil. Righteousness is a quality of God, his *hesed* in election and covenant (loving kindness), and his faithfulness. The word 'truth' in the Bible usually means, not the opposite of error, but of fickleness: the pagan gods were unreliable and could have got out of bed on the wrong side, whereas Israel's God was wholly reliable (truth as opposed to lying). Men and women are righteous because they are Israelites and faithful to the cult, trusting in God, which is a communal idea, not yet much concerned with moral behaviour.

In the story of the wanderings in the desert Israel's trust is the test. In the history of the monarchy the test is faithfulness to the cult and 'adultery' means going after pagan gods away from the bridegroom, God. But the commandments grew in complexity (600 odd in the time of Jesus) and their codification gave rise progressively to the idea of an external code of behaviour as a measure of what keeping the covenant meant.

The idea of personal guilt is at first too spiritual and individualistic. Sin was thought of as communal, as wholly bound up with the consequences; it was corporate and external, or objective rather than subjective. An evil act, such as killing a man, and its consequences were seen as a whole, and as endangering the community. As G. von Rad has written: 'There is nothing in the Old Testament to correspond to the separation we make between sin and penalty.'[5] Hence, sin is public and incriminates the community. Priests decide on whether and how sin could be expiated ritualistically to save the community. If the sin could not be expiated the individual would bear the curse (excommunication, death) to avert it from the people.

So there is a strongly corporate idea of sin: Israel's fate is bound up with the behaviour of its ancestors, and the sins of the fathers. Not until Jeremiah and Ezekiel does the idea of personal responsibility begin to come through (*cf* Jer

31:29–30; Ezek 18:1–30). After the exile the drift towards legalism greatly accentuated, a sign of the power of the priests. (And didn't it all happen again in the Western Church?!). So Christ recalls to the earlier and more basic inspiration of Israel (the Sermon on the Mount), to personal relationship and love as central. Love and sin originate in the heart, we can only learn what love is, and therefore what sin is, from God – not from moral philosophy; sin is a *theological* idea, the rejection of or resistance to God's love, a failure of response. If no grace, then no sin.

Clearly, then, in the Old Testament there is a dominating idea of the solidarity of men and women in sin, and of the effects of one generation's sinfulness on the future. But this does not include the ideas, first, that the single sin of Adam accounts for the subsequent human condition all by itself and, second, that some inner condition of the human soul is passed on by human generation.

Insofar as wisdom and rabbinic literature (200 BC and onwards) reflect on the Adam story, it can be said that if you take Adam to mean man and woman, then certainly our present human condition is the result of man's sin. But the rest of the Old Testament in fact pays scant attention to the Eden story. One of the very few references to it is in Sirach: 'Woman is the origin of sin.' (Sir 25:24). He is a bit of a misogynist!

There are, too, some references in Wisdom (c50 BC): 'It was by the spite of the devil that death entered the world' (Wis 2:24); and 'wisdom saved Adam after his fall [preserved him from its full consequences?] and gave him strength to master all things' (Wis 10:1).

The main idea that comes through is that Adam opened the door to sin, to a force that gained in strength and persuasiveness by being continually added to – *not* that a fixed reality is passed on to all his descendants.

Nature and Grace

The subject 'nature and grace' is one of those vast theological themes which affects all understanding of Christian doctrine, and so of original sin. However, 'nature' and 'grace' are themselves not biblical ideas, as the Bible never considers man apart from his relation to God and the destiny God reveals to man – and that is what 'nature' means.

Here is the difference between Hellenic and Hebraic ways of thought. Man in the Bible is always man before God, man in his relation to God.

New Testament categories for the effect on us of Christ's saving work are: regeneration; recreation; eternal life now; justification; sanctification; divinization; indwelling; sonship; liberation.

The word *charis* in the New Testament mainly means the favour of God. So the angel said to Our Lady, 'Hail the most favoured one.' In the various post-biblical controversies and theories 'grace' came to stand for the various created effects on man of God's saving action; 'nature' for man upon whom God works, or man considered *apart from* God's saving action in Christ.

Augustine's Idea

The chief concern of Augustine in the Pelagian controversy was the gratuity of grace, the need of God's grace for any act of man to be salvific, and this is a moral or psychological understanding of grace. Man's nature and freedom were thought to be severely damaged by original sin: *non posse non peccare, massa damnata*.

Augustine's idea was of *gratia liberatrix*, grace that sets us free. Until scholasticism (that is, for the next seven centuries or more) all the controversies were centred on the mystery of grace and free will, giving rise to such questions as that of predestination.

For Augustine, God's grace is experienced and this was based on his own experience, his hang-ups about sex. What he assumed, and the assumption was never properly looked at, was that only Christians, indeed only orthodox Christians, had the grace of Christ; the rest have not and are lost. So the number of the elect is small. These assumptions persisted. Augustine had to do much juggling with

'God wishes all men to be saved' (1 Tim 2:1–6). The reason he assumed this was that he was convinced that the gratuity of God's grace consisted in his not giving it to everyone, and to some more than others.

Later Scholasticism

I use the word 'later' here because the eventual Tridentine and post-Tridentine doctrine of nature and grace is not in Aquinas in some important respects, though it develops out of Aristotelian categories. It is a metaphysical, rather than a psychological or moral, approach in which God's activity produces an entity, created grace, which led to discussion of how this entity was related to the nature that it 'informs'. It gave rise to the word 'supernatural'.

It is a static model, the growth element being catered for by 'merits'. One might note the tragic severance in the West of dogmatic from ascetical theology, Bernard being the last to hold the two together in one, as for him theology's purpose was to lead to mystical prayer. As a result, the theologians criticize the mystical writers instead of learning from them.

The two-tier presentation made nature and supernature into two separable realities, with infused virtues and supernatural acts laid above the natural ones. This resulted in the elevation of nature to a higher order, with grace 'super added' to nature that can exist without it. Adam lost supernature, and baptism restores it by infusing sanctifying grace. This was in reaction against Luther, showing a swing towards optimism about nature (that is, fallen man). Original sin became an absence of the upper level (original justice), nature was not harmed, the strength of natural reason was stressed.

Various consequences ensued: uncreated grace, God's permanent indwelling, was forgotten in the concentration on created grace as a 'form'; grace becomes a thing, with quantitative increase or loss; and sacraments produce this entity in the soul; grace is not experienced; union with God is seen as effect, not cause; historical fallen man, outside the Church, was progressively identified with 'nature', from which resulted a hostile attitude to other cultures. Man came to be seen as having a natural end, and so arose the concept of limbo; but eventually most of the human race was consigned there, for they could neither go to hell nor heaven, being too primitive to commit sin. This, of course, is completely opposed to the New Testament and makes nonsense of God's design.

Modern Theologies

Ever since the nineteenth century, uncreated grace has been restored as primary, mainly through the work of Moehler and Scheeben, and consequently grace has been thought of in terms of personal relationships. All men receive the grace of Christ, even if we cannot see how and even though they do not know it themselves.

There is room here for some explanation of Rahner, so criticized for his 'anonymous Christians'. God's gift of himself is seen as a constituent of human existence: this is described as a 'supernatural existential', which is not part of nature; the state of pure nature is conceivable, but has never in fact existed. (Conceivable? Such a being would not be human, having no spiritual drive.) This amounts to a reassertion of the view of Augustine and Aquinas that all have a natural desire for God, and so could not possibly have a natural end. If man had no grace he could not sin, sin not being a merely moral word but a rejection of God's grace.

The gratuity of grace lies in God's gift of himself in Christ and in God's initial (to use Augustine's own word[6]) 'drawing' of man, his invitation and call for response. So, there never has been a purely natural man and grace is normal without thereby ceasing to be supernatural, with God's action drawing mankind progressively beyond where the resources of creation, as shared by all other creatures, could take them.

So man is, then, a mystery, a paradox, driven by a divine discontent; he is not fully intelligible to philosophy or to history and can only be fully understood in the light of Christ.

Creation for Christ

The idea has a strong scriptural basis: Paul writes of God's plan 'before the foundation of the world' (Eph 1:4 and 1 Pet 1:20 for example) and of his being 'the first born of all creation, before all things' (Col 1:15 and 1:17).

So grace is God's *first* plan: he created for Christ, just as he created at all to produce Israel. Hence, nature is to be understood within the supernatural, not as a self-contained and intelligible humanity, to which God gratuitously added a further dimension when he need not have done, as a second creation (there was a dispute between Aquinas and Scotists on the point, the latter holding to the view of 'creation for Christ') or because of sin.

The force that draws man to be human is therefore the grace of Christ from the beginning. The gratuity of grace lies in God's initiative throughout to lead man beyond himself: 'nature' becomes a necessary concept for the material on which God works, not for some men as compared with others, nor for some acts or experiences only; and nature is no longer a definably separated constituent, nor a constant.

Dynamic Models

The grace of Christ is essentially dynamic and this model thinks of each of us in terms of growth. It lends itself to an evolutionary view of history and can be combined with the views of Teilhard de Chardin: Christ is the *alpha* and the *omega* and therefore it is the end that explains all that has happened from the beginning, man's origin being explained by its goal. But there are difficulties: *could* man have given a perfect response throughout? Does not the idea of his undeveloped state imply defectiveness as part of God's plan? One envisages God in a dilemma: if he creates there is bound to be sin, and he will be responsible (people always start in the problem of evil by denying that God is responsible for sin; but he is *God*, so of course he is responsible).

Teilhard de Chardin's view was unacceptable to those who had not digested the idea that God's grace is normal without thereby being 'natural'. This makes it possible to consider polygenism (somewhat naively condemned by the Vatican's encyclical *Humani Generis*, published in 1950, which makes one think that popes should not begin encyclicals with the adjective *humanus, -a, um!*).

We become theologically human persons when we are first summoned and stirred by the grace of Christ, and Christian doctrines must be about theological man. This is all remarkably similar to the thought of Irenaeus, a 'Teilhardist' before his time.

Transmission of Moral Weakness

We have looked at the main biblical changes in the idea of sin. We now need to look at other elements in Jewish literature that enter into the thought patterns of the time of the New Testament.

Jewish literature

The elements we are interested in here are those which have some foundation in the canonical Old Testament books, but are chiefly developed in Jewish rabbinical and apocryphal literature, which shows that the centuries immediately before and after the birth of Christ sought to explain the origins of man's sin in three unconnected ways. The following examples from Genesis will clarify this.

GENESIS 6:1–4

Here is a legend of heavenly beings who lusted after the comely daughters of men and produced a race of supermen. Paul's injunction to women to cover their heads in church 'because of the angels' (1 Cor 11:10) has always puzzled commentators; it can only be understood in the light of this passage: that is, the angels are wicked ones who look lovingly on the hair of women in church and could fill them with bad thoughts!

The idea that the demons are the cause of all human depravity is fully worked out in the apocryphal works.[7] Angelology and demonology develop very fully in Jewish apocrypha, in which devils are the cause of all mankind's ills, moral and physical. This is reflected in various ways in the New Testament where illness is treated as diabolic possession *and* treated as the result of sin.

GENESIS 3

Jewish apocrypha develop far more than does the Old Testament idea that sin originated with Adam – an idea developed side-by-side with the previous explanation and as an alternative to it right up to the end of the first century AD.

But, while Adam is referred to as the primary source of sin, and as the cause of death for all, it is repeatedly made clear that we are responsible for our own sins. For example, in Baruch (c100 AD): 'Adam is therefore not the cause save only of his own soul; but each of us has been the Adam of his own soul.'

There is no idea of transmission of sinfulness from father to son by generation, but we are born into a sinful and depraved world in which we suffer from the effects of sin. This is one tradition behind Paul's contrast between Adam and Christ.

GENESIS 6:5 and 8:21

A third explanation is offered by Jewish apocrypha, the *yecer hara* or inclination to evil, which in modern terms we could call libido. It is not connected with the Fall story and is in fact in contrast to it.

In Gen 6:5 there is something in man for which he himself is responsible, whereas in Gen 8:21 it is implied that it is innate. This apparent contradiction runs right through the rabbinical treatment of the subject, and becomes part of technical theology. The rabbis taught that God made the evil *yecer hara* yet man is responsible for controlling and subduing it. But the rabbis did not believe that the evil inclination was transmitted by human generation, for each of us receives it directly from God at generation or birth, and no connection is made with the Fall story.

By contrast with the rabbinical theology, apocryphal literature towards the end of the first century AD is more inclined to connect *yecer hara* and the Fall story. For example, 4 Esdras (an apocryphal book) says that Adam transmits the evil seed in the heart, but it is not made clear whether it is passed on by generation or not. The late date of this work makes it impossible to say how far Paul would have shared his thought, but the whole tradition of the *yecer hara* lies behind Rom 7:13–20.

'Born in Sin'

Throughout the Old Testament there is an awareness of the sinfulness of mankind and, in addition, in one or two places the idea appears that man is 'born in sin', or is a possible interpretation: 'In iniquity was I born and my mother conceived me in sin' (Ps 51:5).

Here the psalmist is deeply conscious of his sin. It is not clear whether this is simply an extreme way of expressing his sinfulness, or whether he is referring to the *yecer hara*, or has some idea of hereditary sinfulness. The second proposition is the most likely, because the psalmist later prays that God will create a clean heart in him to offset the *yecer hara*. Hence, in Job, simply: 'Who can produce the pure from the impure?' (Job 14:4), but in the context of man's birth. And 'no one is clean even when his life is a day old' (LXX). In commenting on the latter, Philo speaks of inherited fate, and the Vulgate even expands to, 'What can make clean that which was conceived from unclean seed?'

The growth of the idea of hereditary taint can be noticed, but it is not there in the New Testament in any clear way, and the reference may again be to the *yecer hara*. Neither text suggests any connection with Adam.

Romans 7

The whole purpose of Romans is to show that all are in the grip of sin, including the Jews, and therefore need redemption by Christ. This faces Paul with the problem of the Law and the Jewish conviction that it was the vehicle of justness and holiness; if not, what was its role?

This question is tackled in Rom 7, Paul personifying sin as a force at work in all of us. The Law is good but did not give the power to obey its own instructions: the 'force of sin' in man made the Law simply an occasion of sinning with a bad conscience. This personification of sin as a force pushing us towards evil may be based on the Jewish tradition of *yecer hara* (for example Rom 7:10–11, 7:12–13, 7:15–17 and 7:22–3). But it may simply be a piece of theological psychology, man's experience of being attracted to sin.

Concupiscence

In Augustine the idea of concupiscence is central: the inability of reason to control the passions and the violence of passion that leads to sin. For him it is the result of original sin or loss of grace (that is, the damage to, or the disintegration of, man's nature that results from inheriting the sin of Adam). This is the sound idea in Augustine's insistence on concupiscence, but he is unsound in tending to identify concupiscence with fleshly desire in general and lust in particular; in regarding it as solely evil. It is only evil when it opposes our destiny, and though he unremittingly calls it evil, Augustine never calls it sin.

The Council of Trent affirmed that concupiscence is not in any true sense sin in the baptized – that was said because Luther was understood as identifying original sin and concupiscence and saying that the baptized were still sinners. Trent does not exclude its being sin in a true and proper sense in the unbaptized and also affirms that it was from sin and led to our actual sins.

For Trent, what is 'formal' about original sin is the loss of holiness and justness. Scholasticism in general taught that concupiscence was a result of original sin, not itself original sin. But Trent does not exclude the idea that concupiscence is the 'material' component of the state in which we are born.

In either case, whereas the originating sin is 'sin' in the full sense, the resulting state can only analogously be called sin – not actual sin – but the flaw in our origin that makes man need the saving grace of Christ.

Forces of Disintegration

It can be seen that the Bible has many elements that could constitute a doctrine of original sin, such as solidarity of man in sin, inclination to evil and Adam's loss of his paradisal state, but they are not a systematic or exact cause-effect doctrine in the scholastic sense. Nor do they attribute man's present sinful state to any one cause. When Adam's sin comes into the picture at all (and there is very little further reference to the story) it is always considered in conjunction with the later sins of mankind.

We have seen that Paul personifies sin as a pervasive force in human experience. He thinks in 'wholes' of experience (unlike any Greek) which illuminate man's stance before God. Apart from Christ we are in the grip of Law-sin-death, and this is what being 'flesh' means.

Paul similarly personifies death (Rom 5). Sin causes not a merely physical death but a death that alienates man from God, a spiritual death. Death so personified comes to mean much the same as sin, a destroying and disintegrating force.

It is interesting to note the explanation of man's state that appears in Athanasius,[8] who is a mixture of Paul and Platonism: man is created with a liability to disintegration (*phthora*) as part of his nature because he is from the dust, but also with a special share in the Logos whereby we participate in the image of God, capable of passing into incorruptibility by 'focusing on God'.

The sin of Adam (turning from God) lets the innate force of disintegration get a grip and weakens man's power to hold to God. So there ensues the progressive grip of destruction because of subsequent sins.

Romans 5:12–21

Oceans of ink have been written on this passage, the whole point of which is to proclaim that Christ alone saves us from sin and from a death that alienates us from God. Christ's saving of all is set against Adam's bringing about their downfall (Rom 5:18) – the Adam-Christ contrast is the key to the passage. God's grace reigns as fully and effectively as sin had done (Rom 5:21).

There is no reason to think that Paul intends to produce a new doctrine of original sin not already contained in the available material, or that he thinks about sin and death in a new cause-effect way that is not to be found in other Jewish or Christian sources.

The passage is bursting with difficulties, not least because Paul starts a sentence he never finishes, but the fact of so many ambiguities shows that no one can draw any particular doctrine of original sin from the passage; and this is a reason why only the bold outlines can be taken as certainly Paul's thought.

There are two traditions behind this passage, that of the 'heavenly man' and sin and death.

THE HEAVENLY MAN

Paul uses the idea of the heavenly man, or heavenly Adam, which is found in Philo. This idea is a Hellenistic interpretation of the two creation accounts found in Genesis, which saw the first as recounting the creation of the ideal Adam, and the second about the real Adam. This is, then, the application of a pagan myth to interpretation of Genesis.

Paul asserts that, so far from heavenly man coming first and being destroyed by demonic forces, the earthly Adam comes first and the heavenly Adam last, the risen Christ (1 Cor 15:47). It is certain that by the first Adam, both in this passage and in Romans, Paul means the concrete Adam, as he had already used this parallelism in 1 Cor 15:21–2 and 15:45–9. He is speaking of the real Adam, but he may be using Adam as a type of all sinners set over against Christ and Christ's body.

ADAM-SIN-DEATH

In Rom 5:12 and the whole passage following it, sin and death mean spiritual forces: Rom 5:17 resuming, 'death established its reign through a single sinner'. Paul is certainly interpreting Genesis according to Wis 2:24, from which the phrase 'death entered the world' is taken. There it is through the devil's spite that sin entered. So he is thinking of a demonic evil force, sin, unleashed by Adam. What Paul does not say is that all men sinned 'in Adam', which interpretation, the commonest among the Latin Fathers, depended on the *in quo* of the Vulgate, which is an impossible translation of the Greek.

What the text means is obscure in the phrase 'because all men sinned'. The wrong translation of *in quo* did more than anything else to establish three ideas not found in Paul: that man's sinful state is due solely to the sin of Adam; that original sin is a standard and uniform state of soul handed on to all by generation; that somehow all are 'contained in' Adam. Nor does 'sinned' in this verse mean that all contracted some inherited sin: the verb is always used for actual sins and cannot be given some strange new meaning here.

In general the doctrine of original sin in this passage can be said to be contained in the causality of Adam, as in the Genesis story and apocrypha. Not, however, in any new sense, nor attributing our sin to Adam's sin, nor with any reference to transmission through generation, and certainly not with the idea of our being 'contained in' Adam or our sins being contained in his.

Trent, to some extent, gives an interpretation of Rom 5:12 that intends the idea, traditional in the West since Augustine, that all sinned in Adam (which the Greek cannot mean). What it aims to exclude by adducing the text is that Adam's sin harmed himself and no one else, and that he caused only death to his posterity and not sin.

Death

In the Old Testament the idea of death is not merely natural, a physical end: Sheol is as far away from God as possible, out of his care (Ps 88:5). In Genesis 2:16–17 it says we must not eat of the tree of good and evil, or else we will die. Hence the basis of the biblical tradition, you will die because of sin.

New Testament theology

We have seen already how Paul theologizes about Gen 2: he personifies death as a force separating man from God, as Adam separated himself from God by his disobedience: sin and death are not readily separable – neither is cause of the other – they are aspects of 'flesh existence' (that is, a process of decadence or corruption leading to death all along). Death, the last enemy, is really the hostile force at work all along. It was *death* that Adam transmitted to his descendants.

But Christ is the true Adam, the true humanity, the true creation for which the old human world existed. *His* death leads to resurrection (Paul), eternal life (John); as baptized we are plunged into his death, we are dead to sin, that is the force that alienates from God (Rom 6:1–11). For John, those who believe have eternal life, the Spirit life now: they have passed from death to life (Jn 5:24).

Systematic Theology

We must understand 'man dies because of sin', not as

something happening in the course of nature that would not otherwise have happened, for man dies because he is of the dust like all animal life.

If you take nature to mean the non-Christian, or man without the grace-storey (super-nature), then it is wholly against the New Testament to say that he is naturally immortal. In 1 Cor 15:45–57 the word *phusikon* is rendered 'physical', but the text says 'psychic': Paul meant by 'body' man before God, who experiences himself both as flesh and as spirit, as weak morally and physically and as open to God's action, a spirit-body and a soul-body (a contradiction to a Greek).

His only hope of life beyond death is in and from the resurrection, and that hope is for the exaltation of *man*. But if man has always been nature and grace then he is in fact immortal and his intimations of mortality are the grace of Christ. With Rahner we can say that ideal man (heavenly Adam) would die but would experience death as transition to eternal life.

Synthetic View

If we combine the view that man was created for Christ with the view that the grace of Christ reaches all, then it follows that the conception of a human being is always more than the start of this worldly life. We can only be understood in terms of the potential God gives us in terms of the deep force that stirs and drives us. We can indicate this by saying that we belong to the supernatural order and can have no end, no resting place, save in the kingdom of Christ. This is the holiness and justness for which he was created and so this is his *fons et origo*, this alone explains him. This is what makes him specifically human.

What stands out most of all from considering evil inclination is that the doctrine is a half truth concentrating only on one side of the reality. Man's force of desire is what it is, has its specific character and more than natural power solely because it is stirred by the grace of Christ, the transforming love of God pressing for unending growth and expansion. So, if there is an inherited sinfulness, there must also be an inherited grace. The traditional doctrines of original sin have concentrated solely on one side of this truth. Man's specifically human power of desire and passion is a power for alienation from God, leading to actual sin, and a power for response to God. It is a spiritual power capable of the sublime and the demonic.

Only modern thought understands heredity and we should not be surprised if, in Christian tradition, the Godward aspects of heredity should be expressed in mythical terms. Through the genetic process we inherit, not just humanity in some standardized form, but a specific mental furniture of propensities, strengths, weaknesses. The psychology of the unconscious teaches us something more about the process of heredity, the inheritance of deep psychic forces that not only identify us with past generations but with each other. The islands join beneath the sea. This brings a profound insight into the solidarity of man in alienation and response, in sin and grace, in Adam and in Christ. As we inherit them, the forces of our spirit are not perfectly integrated, nor absolutely disintegrated, but open to further integration or disintegration, response or alienation. We are not born human or Christian persons but are capable of being made into such by the transforming grace of Christ.

The grace of Christ coming to us from many sources in life is specifically a *redeeming* and reconciling force, and each of us needs to be healed and integrated.

So it restores what Augustine and others over-darkly called the corruption of nature. But even if we had been born wholly integrated, we would still need to be *transformed* from a primitive innocence into mature bearers and sharers of the spirit-life of Christ. The best witnesses are the mystics, Teresa and John of the Cross. Hence the dynamic force of grace in our lives has the twofold aspect of healing and elevation, a viewpoint enabling one to harmonize the moral and ontological approaches to grace, that of Augustine and Aquinas.

Trent, then, asserted that the sin of Adam is one in origin;

is passed on by propagation and not imitation; is in each and proper to each; and can only be removed by the grace of Christ. Theologians have argued that in asserting 'propagation not imitation', Trent wished to insist on the second phrase not the first; and to exclude the idea that man is born simply in holiness and justness, with all the inner forces necessary to reach heaven, and is endangered by the outward pressure towards sin contained in the wicked environment.

P. Schoonenberg reduces original sin to the sin of the world: that would not be adequate to Christian tradition. But he justifies it by a metaphysic in which 'being situated' is an *internal* modification of the being that is situated.[9] One must stress the social dimension of sin in various ways, such as unjust structures of society, the moral air we breathe.

Trent did want to exclude the latter, but we do not need to run away from 'propagation', for we are conceived and born inheriting something of man's alienation from God, but also something of his response.

Clearly, the environment into which a child is born will condition his or her own growing and increasingly more personal response. But, again, for good or ill. At any stage of human development a person is limited by the experience and perspectives of his or her world and society, and can only make a personal response by reference to that environment. But, correspondingly, grace also comes to the person from the outside, from other people, as well as internally from God's gift. More profoundly perhaps than any other source grace comes to man from love of his mother, as she is his environment and matrix. This, more than any other force, integrates man's powers and his growth and enables him to become a person. The fullness of grace and self-understanding is mediated to him by the Church.

It is by reflection on being born into the Church and by Christian marriage that we would need to develop our understanding of how these two sacraments together, of baptism alone in the case of an adult conversion, give to us from outside ourselves the full strength of Christ's grace to fashion us inwardly and to counteract the sinfulness of the world, the environment. Baptism and the other sacraments were separated too much from each other and from the Church in scholastic theology: like a refreshment dispenser, under which you put your cup and obtain drinks of different colours and *effects*.

Trent wished to insist that what we inherit at baptism is an inherent condition of the soul and not simply an environment. This seems to be adequately catered for by the synoptic view here put forward. What is perhaps unusual in this view is the idea that what we inherit is 'proper to each of us' in a way beyond the intentions of Trent. We do not inherit any standard issue, or its absence, but a particular legacy of our own heredity just as we inherit a particular environment.

But the view here presented is unusual in asserting that we inherit not only the effects of sin but also the effects of grace. We are neither totally in the power of the devil nor totally out of it, and this goes some way towards solving the problem of the unbaptized infant, who in the former view belonged neither to heaven nor hell. Concentration on the negative side of our inheritance envisaged us totally outside the field of redeeming grace, labelled for hell and inevitably destined to buy our ticket there the moment we were old enough to choose between good and evil. Do we not rather have to say that we are born for heaven, though capable of developing a power of rejection? That Christ's love is stronger than the grip of evil? That death is swallowed up in victory?

The dogma of the Immaculate Conception is one that is difficult to understand at this point in the Church's theology because of our groping for a new view of what Our Lady is free *from*. The dogma is that she was preserved by a singular privilege from every *stain* of original sin (for example, concupiscence), not that she committed no sins.

My presentation has urged that no one is conceived simply with the sin-force as part of their inheritance, and not also the grace-force; it seems, then, to be in danger, not of denying her condition before God at conception, but of extending it to everyone and therefore denying her any singular privilege.

In reply I can only tentatively suggest that her privilege must always be understood in terms of the role for which God cast her in his plans of creating a world for Christ. Incidentally, the idea of Immaculate Conception originated in a treatise of Anselm, which was using a medical metaphor, for no other way was seen of preserving Christ from original sin. Indeed, because of Jesus' saying that John the Baptist was the greatest among men, he too was thought to have been free from original sin, and hence *his* mother must also have been free (how far back do you go?!)

If we stand back from this synoptic view of Jesus and original sin, we find that Christ and sin are pervasive forces in human experience, and if we have to say that sin is inevitable we have to go on to say that it is only creation for Christ that makes us capable of sinning. That is why God cares and is loving and merciful to the sinner. We do not first understand sin and then grasp the meaning of redemption but, as Karl Barth insisted, it is only in knowing that we are redeemed from sin that we know we are sinners. It is only in understanding Christ that we understand Adam.

The doctrine of original sin has concentrated too exclusively on half of what God's revelation tells us, on man's solidarity in sin. It has at times tried to understand Adam apart from Christ. But even more mysterious is our solidarity in grace and the judgment God passes, not on separated individuals, but on all of us, his creation for Christ. 'For in making all mankind prisoners to disobedience God's purpose was to show mercy to all' (Rom 1:32).

16

Just War Forsooth

The just war theory which has for so long guided Christian moral judgment has had the most profoundly pernicious effects in Christian history. There are at least three grave errors in the theory, which can be succinctly pointed out.

First, it offends against one of the most elementary principles of justice that anyone should be judge in their own cause. And yet throughout the history of the idea it has been precisely in their own cause that people have used the theory – and have invariably come to the conclusion that they were right to fight. Often opposing sides have done so, without either even considering seeking an uninvolved arbiter.

Second, matters of moral dilemma or difficult decision are not those where all is white on one side and black on the other, where in fact no decision is needed. It is always a question of grey areas; always a question of trying to discern the balance of good and evil; and very often (as surely was the case in the Gulf War) there is no good in sight anywhere, just a dire necessity to prevent even greater evil. But, if you apply the word 'just' to actions which are in no sense good, even if they are seen as here and now necessary and therefore right, the effect almost inevitably is that *any* means are then considered justified, and the most appalling actions are carried out with the blanket idea of justice spread over them: almost sanctimoniously. You cannot fight with one hand tied behind your back, and the job has to be got over with as fast and as thoroughly as possible. Then we can celebrate a deserved victory. God was obviously on our side.

The third is perhaps only the theological dimension or extension of the second. So far from considering ourselves just when we resort to fighting as an inevitable and right course of action in the face of great threat, we should do so in fear and trembling, in fear of the judgment of God, and begging his forgiveness for the drastic and deeply tragic situation that forces upon us such sub-human and destructive activity. David Jenkins has written:

> It is absolutely essential to retain the conviction that acts which are dehumanising, inhuman and less than fully human, remain precisely that even when they are politically essential or inevitable, or at least, held to be so. The attitude of the oppressed in hating his oppressor and the act of the oppressed in imprisoning, terrorizing or killing his oppressor do not become human and humanizing because they are part of a historical process of liberation, which liberation may, as a whole, be held to be just, justified and hopeful.[1]

It is surely outrageous to call any war 'just' – particularly for a Christian. Christian warfare used to be against the devil in ourselves. Then it was thought to be justified against the Turk, especially if he threatened our way of life and persecuted our Church. (No turning the cheek with Turks!)

Then war was justified (by both sides) when Christian fought Christian. How very far from the teaching and lifestyle of Jesus!

The alternative is not pacifism (which is a form of prophecy, but also a form of opting out of responsibility) but humility and recognition of how far the human race still is from being human.

Here, 'The Gospel' of R. S. Thomas jolts us:

> *And in the midst of council*
> *a bittern called from the fen*
> *outside. A sparrow flew in*
> *and disappeared through the far doorway.*
> *'If your faith can explain . . . ' So*

they were baptised, and the battles began
for the kingdom of this world. Were
you sent, sparrow? An eagle
would have been more appropriate,
some predator to warn them
of the ferocity of the religion
that came their way. The fire was not more voluble
than the blood that would answer the sword's
question.

Charles by divine right
king. And not all our engines can drain
Marston Moor. The bittern
is silent now. The ploughshares are beaten
to guns and bombs. Daily we publish
hurrying with it to and fro on steel
wings, the good news of the kingdom.[2]

And, be it noted, it's the men who fight and involve
everyone in their fighting in this brutal physical way – and
then produce high-sounding rationalizations to justify and
canonize decisions they have already made from their guts
and muscles.

17

Authority

In recent years 'authority' has been a very live issue within the Roman Catholic Church, both internally and in inter-Church relations. Internally there have been much publicized cases of central authority endeavouring to clamp down on theologians of various kinds (doctrinal, moral, broadly 'liberation' writers), and on the political involvement of clergy. And there have been the much more diffused questions about consultation, delegation, decision making, 'subsidiarity', in the day-to-day running of regions, dioceses, parishes. Externally, the exercise of authority has been a central issue in discussions and negotiations for unity between different Christian traditions. Baptists are among those whose life is focused on the local Church membership, and who resist any idea of higher 'Church' authority. The subject has been central to Anglican and Roman Catholic efforts to reach agreement: their treatment of authority has been diffuse and somewhat elusive, and has left the matter of papal authority ultimately unsolved.

This is a complex matter and in this chapter I attempt to distinguish different aspects of it and then, by focusing these aspects, place them in the life of the Church.

Components of Authority

One may begin with the very general observation that authority is a constituent of very varied forms of human society. A form of human society (a family, for example) does not first exist and then have authority (in this case parental) added 'over' it: it can only exist with authority as a constituent element of it.

Constitutive of Society

It is impossible to think of a form of human society without any component of authority: there would only be an aggregate of individuals. The Church did not first exist – logically, or chronologically or theologically – and then have authority added over it. It was from the outset a structured society, with a pastoral ministry of some with regard to the rest.

Human forms of society are extremely diverse. One might take as examples a family, a business firm, a football team, an army, a civil state. Because of their differences, the exact part played by authority in each, its nature and its appropriate exercise, will be very different. But in each case authority is a constituent element of the society, which could not be itself without it.

One must, therefore, banish any idea that authority essentially inhibits human society and blocks its self-realization. Inappropriate exercise of authority can certainly do this; but of itself authority exists to enable any form of human society to be fully itself and to fulfil its duties.

Responsibility for Others

There can be no authority without responsibility for others: it is a personal relationship arising from such responsibility. If one's role is simply to carry out the will and decisions of others, then one is simply an executive, responsible to others but not for them; one has no authority.

Most discussions of Church authority today fail to mention responsibility, and are often very cloudy in consequence. Perhaps as a reaction against autocratic forms, or exercise, of authority, the talk has tended to be about 'service', as if to suggest that the one holding authority is in no way 'above' others. Certainly, the holding of authority is a ministry in the Church, and so is a service (which is what 'ministry' means). And certainly, too, there are honoured precedents for the word, as in the title claimed by the bishops of Rome since Gregory the Great, *servus servorum Dei*. Above all other precedents, Jesus himself said he had not come to be served but to serve and to give his life as a ransom for many.

So, service must characterize the aim and attitude of anyone holding authority in the Church – rather than, say, the seeking of honour or of power over the lives of others. And this aim and attitude should therefore pervade the style of authority's exercise. Finally, anyone who has held a position of authority has been acutely aware of the responsibility for others which such a position involves, and of the essential loneliness of that responsibility: this is the desk on which the buck stops. There is no one behind you, to whom you can pass on the responsibility; you must carry it yourself. To carry responsibility for others is certainly a service to them – though not all service to others carries responsibility for them.

To consider authority in terms of responsibility raises the further question: *to whom* is the one with authority responsible or answerable? In a political democracy the head of the government is answerable to the whole society for which he or she is responsible: the people are entitled, not only to criticize the exercise of authority, but ultimately to renew or remove the authority, and to reward or punish its use.

But not all forms of human society are democracies, nor should they try to be. Parents are not ultimately answerable to their children for their exercise of authority over them: they are in some respects answerable to society for the fulfilment of their responsibilities, but in the last resort they are answerable only to God.

The Church is not a political democracy, nor indeed any other form of merely political association or organization. It is the Body of Christ, the community in which the Lord lives and acts. Hence, to hold authority in the Church is to serve and mediate the Lordship of Christ, and its proper exercise should at every point be governed by this fact. The pastor is, to be sure, open to advice and criticism of those for whom he or she is responsible, but in the last resort is answerable only to the Lord.

The pastor's service of others is service of Christ the Lord as he exists in those who believe in and are committed to him.

The ways in which authority should be exercised, and responsibility for others fulfilled, will vary very much according to the type of human society in question and the purposes for which it exists. There can be no single model. What might be appropriate for, say, an army in wartime, could obviously defeat the aims of a school or a firm or a football team. There can be points of comparison, greater or fewer, between different types of society; but each is ultimately itself and different from the others, and the appropriate exercise of authority needs to be carefully discerned in each case, with the nature and aims of the society firmly in view.

It is important to emphasize that the responsibility entailed by authority is always for others as human persons. It can never be simply for some goal, some sub-human end-product. A commercial firm should not be managed simply to make a profit: management has responsibilities of different kinds for all involved in the firm, and to society at large. It cannot be the responsibility of a religious superior simply to see that the rules are observed: the responsibility must always be for the development of persons in a community of faith. The repeated clashes of Jesus with 'the authorities' of Judaism arose out of his assertion of the priority of people over laws – 'the sabbath was made for man, and not man for the sabbath' (Mk 2:27).

As long as responsibility is for others as people, and not simply for some definable end-product, then it must be limited.

Authority can only do its best to ensure that others can do their best; it can only create the conditions in which it is possible for others to play a full part in fulfilling the aims of the society in question.

Power and dependence

However much we may be inclined to shy away from the word, one cannot be responsible unless in some way or another one has the power to carry out the responsibility. 'Power' here may mean no more than possibility, freedom of action. The kind of power and its appropriate exercise will vary greatly from one form of society to another. It is not of itself a matter of force or constraint, but that of being in the position to take decisions affecting others which those others will accept, such as the appointment of personnel, or the demarcation of the functions and responsibilities of others. In a society such as the Church, in view of its nature and aims, decisions are best taken collegially. But the one in authority or with final responsibility is able to create (or to stifle) the conditions in which a common mind can emerge. And, at the end of the day, when all points of view have been aired but consensus as to relative values has not emerged, he or she may well have to take the decision. It can be a difficult tightrope to walk: for example, if one lets the airing of views run on indefinitely, there will be complaints that progress is impeded because 'the man at the top' can never make up his mind; if one decides that consultation has exhausted itself and makes a decision, some people will inevitably say: 'His mind was made up in advance, and he never really listens.'

Compliance or dependence in some form on the part of those under authority is the necessary correlative to the power or ability to exercise responsibility. If a school, for example, is to function coherently in order to achieve its purpose, then pupils and teachers need to comply with the decisions and dispositions of the head teacher. In the Church, as it is a community of faith, obedience can only be 'the obedience of faith'; that is, it must always be obedience to Christ whose lordship is mediated by those in authority. But the two do not coincide, as the human authority can never perfectly mediate Christ's lordship; and it can certainly never substitute for it. For most purposes, in view of the limitations of the human condition, and in recognition of the limits of one's own convictions and point of view, one gives obedience to human authority 'as to the Lord'. But the situation can arise in which the claim of obedience to the Lord makes it impossible to accept the decision of the human authority.

The word 'power' meets with resistance because of its overtones of enforcement or sanctions. But this is a quite separate matter, needing to be examined separately for every form of human society. Parents with young children may well need to employ rewards and punishments, or at any rate disincentives, to ensure that their children develop patterns of behaviour necessary for their own good. But the whole art of parenthood is to help children interiorize right decisions, as they become increasingly responsible for their own lives, and so progressively to relax external constraints. Whether any sort of enforcement is appropriate in the Church, as a community of faith, is very doubtful. Encouragement and assistance of every kind are obviously appropriate, to enable Christians to live fully responsible lives in and for the good of their community. But you cannot force people to live by faith, or by love, and any attempt to do so is almost certain to be self-defeating. From the earliest days there has been the ultimate sanction of excommunication or cutting off from the community. But it can be, and has been, far too lightly invoked and thereby trivialized. Communion means sharing, and to excommunicate anyone is not a matter of casting them out, but of declaring that, by views or actions which are fundamentally incompatible with the aims and ideals of the society, they have put themselves outside it.

Respect

Finally, something in the nature of respect for the person in authority goes with all positions of responsibility. This is a very un-legal and unclassifiable area.

The Latin word *auctoritas* carries more of the aura of respect (dignity, prestige) than the more legal word 'authority'. The military dictator, Octavian, who eventually gained control of Rome after the assassination of Julius Caesar, took the title 'Augustus' so as to lay claim to the veneration of the senate and the people of Rome and their subject peoples. The title derives from the same root as *auctoritas*. By contrast, Jesus warned his followers against this style:

> The kings of the gentiles lord it over them; and those in authority over them style themselves 'benefactors' [the practice of many Syrian kings who had lorded it over Israel]. But not so with you; rather let the greatest among you become as the youngest, and the leader as one who serves . . . I am among you as one who serves' (Lk 22:25–7).

And in the ecumenical discussion it emerges clearly that the objection of the so-called non-espiscopal Churches to episcopacy is not to the overall functions of responsibility exercised by bishops (which they exercise themselves under other names), but to the trappings of prelacy which accumulated round Church leaders in feudal times.

Respect will, however, be given to one in authority in the Church, in that he is seen as serving and mediating the lordship of Christ. But, as in any authority situation, the degree to which anyone commands respect for himself (as opposed to regard for his office) is a matter of what today we call 'charisma'; a matter of how far he or she manifests the requisite qualities of responsible leadership. And as in any authority situation, if people have to appeal to their office or status, its a sure sign that they lack the gifts.

Authority and Law

The nature of a particular form of authority, and the scope of its responsibilities may well need to be expressed in constitutional law, and supported for its satisfactory exercise by further regulation. Defining the scope and exercise of authority both limits that authority and enables people to know where they stand.

But this is not necessarily so, as the case of parental authority makes clear. And where, as in the United Kingdom, there is no written constitution, what is constitutional or unconstitutional is a matter of precedent or consensus, something open to gradual development and subtle shifts.

It is not law which constitutes authority: it is the nature, values and aims of a society which do that. The extent to which any given society may wish to express its patterns of responsibility and organization in laws is a matter of choice. Laws are a means to an end. As a society develops in history and enters into new situations, modifying its own values and altering its relations to other societies, it will constantly need to change its constitutional and other laws. Laws reflect the consciousness of society; they cannot dictate to it.

This needs to be said clearly of the Church, particularly in view of the dominance of the idea of law in Europe from the twelfth century onwards. Before the rise of true ecclesiology (theology of the Church) in the twentieth century, there were many attempts in Roman Catholic post-Reformation thinking to define the Church in terms of constitutional or political theory, of its nature secular. But that cannot be done, because the Church is never simply a human society: it is always 'the mystery' of God's action, the people in whom Christ dwells and acts by his Spirit to establish his kingdom in all his creation. At any given time there may be value in, or need for, the Church to express the structure of its authority in law. But any such expression is essentially conditioned by transitory historical and cultural factors and cannot be timeless or binding for the indefinite future.

The ministry of authority in the Church is a ministry of responsibility, both towards the members of the Church and towards the rest of the human family – that *both* may grow more and more into Christ's kingdom. And perception of this task and dual responsibility are always changing, as they have always changed throughout history. How else could there be any growth towards Christ's kingdom? Thus, even a cursory glance at the papacy will show that, after its emergence in the course of the first four or five centuries it has continued to be subject to constant development. It has *de facto* served as a focus or centre of unity in a worldwide Church, and from this fact its central responsibility can be discerned. How it has fulfilled or attempted to fulfil that role in the past is a matter of very varied history. Between the Council of Trent and Vatican II the papacy became an increasingly dominating form of central government, maintaining unity by enforcing uniformity, even upon the new Churches of Asia and Africa. But at Vatican II new insights broke through, and even exploded, into view. It is very significant that the first Constitution it handled was that on the Sacred Liturgy, in which the variety and richness of Christian tradition began to get recognition, and the ideal of uniformity within the Church was abandoned. At the same time the values expressed in other Christian traditions were recognized, and the duty of uniting Christians became apparent and received open expression. So today the challenge facing the papacy is how to be a ministry of unity precisely among very varied and sometimes contrasting forms of Christian life and expression. How that responsibility can best be fulfilled in our own time must be a matter of careful discernment, of patient and prayerful evaluation of the 'spirits' and voices that are abroad, in order that the unitive guidance of Christ's Spirit may be heard and followed. That challenge certainly cannot be met by appealing to past precedents and patterns, considered appropriate for the ministry of unity as it was then conceived.

Authority in the Church

Discussions on authority in the Church have concentrated almost exclusively on the responsibilities and consequent authority of the ordained ministry. It was to the merit of N. Lash that he broadened the issue in his book, *Voices of*

Authority (1976). Developing an idea found in Newman, Lash wrote of the 'three voices of authority, those of the pastor, the theologian (or scholar), and the saint (or prophet)'.[1]

These three voices are not to be thought of as separate classes of persons, but as distinct *loci* or sources of authority – voices commanding attention. A pastor may well be a scholar, or speak with a prophetic voice. In the patristic age the great thinkers and writers who developed the Church's expression of her faith were mainly bishops. In our own day bishops such as Helder Camara and Oscar Romero have spoken out with strongly prophetic voices to challenge both civil governments and Christian pastors over their support for unjust social structures. For example, Robert Murray has shown that the over-identification of ordained ministry with priesthood in the Catholic tradition has obscured the prophetic role which essentially belongs to ordained ministry in its service of Jesus, not only as 'Founder' of the Christian community, but as 'Challenger' of establishments both ecclesiastical and secular.[2]

The responsibilities of the pastor as such are for the whole life of the Christian community over which he presides. He has to be mainly concerned with the workings of 'the system' in all its complexities: the welfare and spiritual vitality of all his assistant ministers; the nourishment of all the faithful by 'word' and sacraments, so that their gifts may be developed and used in the Church's mission in and to the world; the fitting celebration of divine worship in the Church's liturgy; the spiritual formation and intellectual training of future ministers; and provision of all the material resources which these responsibilities involve. And in addition he is constantly looked to for guidance on the pressing social and moral issues of the day.

The scholar, by contrast, does not carry general responsibility for the life of the community. As he seeks to give contemporary expression to the Christian faith, he is certainly responsible to that faith and to the tradition in which he has received it. And he is responsible for the intellectual integrity and accuracy of his discipline. His work will be very largely of an exploratory and pioneering kind, out on the frontiers of the Church as it were, as he endeavours to relate the plurality of Christian tradition to new insights and situations, and often to new problems of which the Church at large will still be unaware.

It is thus inevitable, and it is for the good of the Church, that there should be some tension between the pastor and the scholar – a tension which may exist within the same person. It is inevitable insofar as the theologian will challenge received ways of understanding and instructing, in order to lead them forward to a renewed and deeper expression. Without this renewal the Church's message will become increasingly out of touch with the preoccupations of contemporary people. It will no longer speak to the questions they actually ask or relate to the world and to life as they experience it; it will use a language, drawn from former world views and their attendant problems, which people no longer understand. The role of the pastor however, will tend to be one of conserving and protecting, of witnessing to the already acquired insights of the Church. With his concern for the faith and understanding of the whole community, he will question whether new ideas are in continuity with the Church's self-understanding, a true development of doctrine, or a break with and a betrayal of it.

It is essential for the good of the Church that this tension should exist, and should be sustained and lived rather than resolved. It ensures the cumulative character of Christian theology. Without it, the Church would either be blown about by every wind of doctrine (*cf* Eph 4:14), amid general bewilderment, uncertain of its message; or, robbed of vision and of the life-giving power of creative imagination, would endlessly repeat dead formulas falling on deafer and deafer ears. Hence it is naive for either theologian or pastor to be hurt or surprised at any tension that arises between them; and it is extremely harmful for either to usurp, or set aside, or attempt to suppress the role of the other. Each needs to respect and as far as possible to support the other's role.

In fact, throughout the centuries, the theologians have exercised the *magisterum*, have been the teachers in and of the Church. And in very many cases, of which Thomas Aquinas was a notable example, their presentation has at first met with a strong resistance. The intellectual apostolate is truly an apostolate, carried on in and for the Church. And it has characteristically borne the marks of a following of Jesus, not only in its inherent difficulties but in opposition and frustration, and often in temporary eclipse and failure. The process of evaluation and assimilation by the Church as a whole is often a long one, before what began as teaching 'in' the Church gains various forms of recognition and becomes teaching 'of' the Church. An outstanding example in our own day has been the work of Yves Congar, who often challenged prevailing attitudes and assumptions – about tradition, about the role of the laity, and about the divisions between Christians – and whose views finally came to underlie many of the pronouncements of Vatican II, thus becoming part of the *magisterium* of the bishops.

So far I have considered the pastor and the scholar as sources of authority in the Church, or criteria of Christian truth. But a third 'voice' was indicated by Lash in the wake of Newman, that of 'the saints'.[3] In the first place this draws attention to the fact that Christ dwells by his Spirit in all his faithful, and not only in pastors or those with special education and teaching function. They, too, have a contribution to make to the Church's contemporary expression of its faith. This *locus* of authority has mainly been considered in Catholic tradition in terms of the 'consent of the faithful', or reception of teaching. And this is certainly an element in the part played by the committed faithful. Negatively, if what is propounded by pastor or scholar as the right teaching about human and Christian living seems to the committed faithful to be unreal, and out of touch with the realities of human experience (in marriage, for example), then this is surely a sign that the teaching in question is at least inadequate. Positively, if new orientations in liturgy or in relations with other Christian communions, for example, at once capture the imagination of 'the saints', ring the bell with them, formulate what in their heart of hearts they have always wanted or known to be the case, then this is surely a sign that the voice of the Spirit in the Church has truly been heard and expressed. But the role of ratifying, supporting and translating into effect what has been proposed by others does not exhaust the voice of the committed faithful. They also have a part to play in setting the agenda, if not the leading part. It has been the merit of those broadly called 'liberation theologians' to bring out that it is the voices of the deprived and oppressed that have forced pastors and scholars to rethink the whole framing of the Good News about Christ and about the Church's role in building his kingdom. The question, 'What is Christian faith to them?', urgently demands an answer.

Again, in all parts of the world the voices of women are raised about their second-class status and the neglect of the gifts which Christ's Spirit has given them.

In parts of the Church where there is an acute shortage of priests, the whole absorption of the Church's ministry by the full-time ordained male ministry is being called into question, forcing the theology of ministry to be wholly refashioned. And, to refer to an example given in an earlier chapter of this book, the experience of couples in inter-Church marriages speaks loudly from the place of involvement and of commitment about traditional approaches to Eucharistic sharing.

Thus the enterprise of theology, or of enunciating Christian truth, is seen to operate between three poles. There is not only the biblically-based tradition of doctrine, guarded by the pastor. Nor have we to add only the efforts of the scholar to relate this tradition to the new insights and problems of a constantly changing world. The living faith of the saints, the people of God, is where both pastor and scholar start, the lived experience of encountering Christ in his people which all have inherited. It is this living faith which both pastor and scholar are called on to interpret and enunciate in the light both of the received tradition and of new challenges.

Notes

Chapter 1: *Origin of the Gospels*

1. C. H. Dodd, *According to the Scriptures* (Collins 1961).
2. Now held in Manchester University archives.
3. J. A. T. Robinson, *The Body* (SCM Press 1976).
4. R. Bultmann, *The Gospel of John* (Blackwell 1971). See also his *Jesus Christ and Mythology* (SCM Press 1970).
5. M. Hengel, *Studies in the Gospel of Mark* (SCM Press 1985).
6. W. H. Kelber, *Mark's Story of Jesus* (Fortress Press 1979).
7. B. Vawter, *This Man Jesus* (Chapman 1973).
8. W. Vanstone, *The Stature of Waiting* (Darton, Longman & Todd 1982).
9. The Greek word means both 'betray' and 'hand over'.
10. J. A. T. Robinson, *The Priority of John* (SCM Press 1985).
11. R. Brown, *The Gospel According to John*, Vol. I (Doubleday, New York, 1966 and 1971).
12. Docetic: the view that he was only an appearance of God.
13. R. Bultmann, *The Gospel of John* (Blackwell 1971).
14. LXX: the Septuagint, the Greek translation of the Old Testament.
15. W. Wrede, *The Messianic Secret*. (The German original was published in 1901. Et Cambridge and London 1981.)
16. J. Fitzmyer, 'The Resurrection of Jesus Christ according to the New Testament', in *The Month* (November 1987). This article has been helpful in preparing this section on the Resurrection.

Chapter 2: *Ecclesiology*

1. R. Bultmann, *Jesus Christ and Mythology* (SCM Press 1970).

2. Tertullian: *De Baptisimo*.
3. Cyprian: *De Unitate Ecclesiae*.
4. R. Bultmann, *The Gospel of John* (Blackwell 1971).
5. Lesslie Newbigin, *The Gospel in a Pluralist Society* (SCM Press 1987), p. 107.
6. Gerhard Lohfink's farewell address published in *Theology Digest*, Vol. 36, n. 2.
7. In what follows I am indebted to Avery Dulles and his book, *Models of the Church* (Gill & Macmillan 1976).
8. K. Barth: *Church Dogmatics* (T. & T. Clark 1981).
9. Pius XII, *Darkness Over the Earth* (Vatican Press 1939).
10. In what follows I am indebted to John Thornhill and his book, *Sign and Promise* (Collins 1988).
11. H. de Lubac, *Catholicism* (Burns Oates 1950).
12. H. de Lubac, *The Church, Paradox and Mystery* (Ecclesia Press 1969).
13 John Thornhill, *Sign and Promise* (Collins 1988), p. 79.

Chapter 3: *New Testament Christology*

1. B. Vawter, *This Man Jesus* (Chapman 1973).
2. *Similitudes of Enoch* and *Testaments of XII Patriarchs*.
3. R. Bultmann, *Jesus Christ and Mythology* (SCM Press 1970).
4. Ibid.
5. The latter is confirmed by its use in the Eucharistic liturgy, the Didache 10:6.

Chapter 4: *Baptism, Eucharist, Penance*

1. M. Thurian, *The Eucharistic Memorial* (Lutterworth Press 1960).
2. *Cf* the Anglican-Roman Catholic International Commission, *Agreed Statement on the Eucharist* (SPCK and Catholic Truth Society 1972).
3. Hippolytus: *The Apostolic Tradition*.
4. Tertullian: *De Baptismo*.
5. Cyril of Jerusalem: *On the Mysteries*.
6. Justin: *First Apology*, 66.

Chapter 5: *A Good Conscience*

1. Teilhard de Chardin, *The Phenomenon of Man* (Collins 1964).
2. I. Kant: *Critique of Practical Reason*.
3. J. Fletcher, *Situation Ethics* (SCM Press 1966).
4. *Decree on Ecumenism* (Vatican II 1964).
5. Ibid., n.2.

Chapter 6: *Atonement*

1. G. Aulen, *Christus Victor* (SPCK 1965).
2. Augustine: *City of God*, Book X.
3. *Cur Deus Homo?*

Chapter 7: *Our God Reigns*

1. The following points are a digest of Gerhard Lohfink's farewell address (mentioned earlier: see n. 6, Chapter 2) and not a verbatim account.
2. Lesslie Newbigin, *The Other Side of 1984* (World Council of Churches 1990). I greatly admire Newbigin's writing, which I only came across recently.
3. D. Jenkins, *The Contradiction of Christianity* (SCM Press 1976), pp. 37–8.
4. Ibid.

Chapter 8: *First Corinthians*

1. I have used the RSV translation throughout this chapter.
2. 'Chloe' is the Greek for 'Green'.
3. C. H. Dodd, *According to the Scriptures* (Collins 1961).
4. And found in the Liturgy of the Didache (Teaching of the Apostles, c95AD).

Chapter 10: *Body Theology*

1. I have used the RSV translation throughout this chapter.
2. J. A. T. Robinson, *The Body* (SCM Press 1966).
3. J. Coventry, *Reconciling* (SCM Press 1985).

4. H. de Lubac, *Corpus Mysticum* (Aubier Press, Paris, 1944).
5. Cyprian: *Letter to Magnus*.
6. Ignatius of Antioch to the Ephesians.

Chapter 11: *Spirituality*

1. P. Brown, *The Body and Society: Men, Women and Sexual Renunciation in Early Christianity* (Faber & Faber 1988).
2. A. de Mello, *Sadhana* (Anand Press, India, 1978).
3. On this tendency, see the books of Esther de Waal and note the pervasive Trinitarian character of the prayer: *cf* E. de Waal, *The Celtic Vision* (Darton, Longman & Todd 1988) and *A World Made Whole* (Collins 1991).
4. Rosemary Haughton, *The Passionate God* (Darton Longman & Todd 1981).
5. Origen is here being quoted in P. Brown, *The Body and Society: Men, Women and Sexual Renunciation in Early Christianity* (Faber & Faber 1988).

Chapter 12: *Sharing Communion*

1. M. Finch and R. Reardon, *Sharing Communion* (Harper Collins 1983). I am grateful to Harper Collins for permission to base this chapter on those Conclusions.
2. *Decree on Ecumenism* (1964).
3. *Decree on the Eastern Catholic Churches* (1964).
4. *Decree on Ecumenism* (1964).
5. *Ecumenical Directory* (1967).
6. Ibid., n.55.
7. *Instruction* (1972).
8. *Interpretative Note* (1973).
9. *Constitution on the Liturgy* (1963).

Chapter 14: *Paul on Sin*

1. Rom 5:12 in the RSV translation. My italics.
2. My translation of Rom 5:12. My italics.

Chapter 15: *Original Sin Revisited*

1. D. Hick, *God and the Universe of Faiths* (Macmillan 1988).
2. Ibid.
3. Elizabeth Sarah, 'The biblical account of the first woman: a Jewish feminist perspective', in Teresa Elwes (ed.) *Women's Voices* (Marshall Pickering 1992).
4. 'Aetiological': *aitia* is the Greek for 'cause'.
5. G. von Rad, *Old Testament Theology* (SCM Press 1965).
6. In Augustine's *Treatises on John*, 26.
7. The *Book of Enoch* (*c*150 BC) and, similarly, in the book of *Jubilees* (*c*150 BC) and also in *Reuben* (late second century BC).
8. Athanasius: *On the Incarnation of the Word*.
9. P. Schoonenberg, *Man and Sin* (Sheed & Ward 1965).

Chapter 16: *Just War Forsooth*

1. D. Jenkins, *The Contradiction of Christianity* (SCM Press 1976), p. 68.
2. R. S. Thomas, 'The Gospel', *Later Poems* (Macmillan 1984), p. 207.

Chapter 17: *Authority*

1. N. Lash, *Voices of Authority* (Sheed & Ward 1976), especially Chapter 7.
2. R. Murray, 'Prophecy, Politics and Priesthood', in *The Month* (October 1987)
3. N. Lash, *Voices of Authority* (Sheed & Ward 1976), especially Chapter 7.